The Palgrave Kets de Vries Library

Manfred F. R. Kets de Vries, Distinguished Professor of Leadership and Development and Organizational Change at INSEAD, is one of the world's leading thinkers on leadership, coaching, and the application of clinical psychology to individual and organizational change.

Palgrave's professional business list operates at the interface between academic rigor and real-world implementation. Professor Kets de Vries's work exemplifies that perfect combination of intellectual depth and practical application and Palgrave is proud to bring almost a decade's worth of work together in the Palgrave Kets de Vries Library.

Manfred F. R. Kets de Vries

The Path to Individual and Organizational Transformation

Confronting the Elephant in the Room

Manfred F. R. Kets de Vries
Paris, France

ISSN 2730-7581   ISSN 2730-759X (electronic)
The Palgrave Kets de Vries Library
ISBN 978-3-031-88329-3   ISBN 978-3-031-88330-9 (eBook)
https://doi.org/10.1007/978-3-031-88330-9

© The Editor(s) (if applicable) and The Author(s), under exclusive license to Springer Nature Switzerland AG 2025

This work is subject to copyright. All rights are solely and exclusively licensed by the Publisher, whether the whole or part of the material is concerned, specifically the rights of reprinting, reuse of illustrations, recitation, broadcasting, reproduction on microfilms or in any other physical way, and transmission or information storage and retrieval, electronic adaptation, computer software, or by similar or dissimilar methodology now known or hereafter developed.
The use of general descriptive names, registered names, trademarks, service marks, etc. in this publication does not imply, even in the absence of a specific statement, that such names are exempt from the relevant protective laws and regulations and therefore free for general use.
The publisher, the authors and the editors are safe to assume that the advice and information in this book are believed to be true and accurate at the date of publication. Neither the publisher nor the authors or the editors give a warranty, expressed or implied, with respect to the material contained herein or for any errors or omissions that may have been made. The publisher remains neutral with regard to jurisdictional claims in published maps and institutional affiliations.

Cover illustration: image by Vinogradov Oleg | Shutterstock

This Palgrave Macmillan imprint is published by the registered company Springer Nature Switzerland AG
The registered company address is: Gewerbestrasse 11, 6330 Cham, Switzerland

If disposing of this product, please recycle the paper.

Foreword

Childhood memory: *Morning birdsong outside my window, my chest swells with hope and excitement. At the break of day, anything is possible.*

The Importance of Hope

I am very honored to be asked to write the foreword to my father's book. This work introduces readers to the psychodynamic-systemic methodology (also known as the clinical approach) that he and his colleagues have developed through their work with leaders, teams, and organizations. The book offers practical guidance while inviting other practitioners to adopt and advance this approach to create positive change.

Through my work as a consultant and coach, I have witnessed how this approach drives meaningful change. It awakens hope in people, showing them that progress is within reach. This sense of possibility empowers them to imagine a better future, even in the face of uncertainty and challenges.

There is a centuries-old Dutch saying—"*hoop doet leven*"—which means "hope sustains life." Although its origins are lost to time, it captures a fundamental truth about human existence. Hope is much more than mere optimism. While optimism assumes that good things will happen regardless of our actions, hope acknowledges future uncertainty while still motivating us to act. The *Stanford Encyclopedia of Philosophy* defines hope as a multifaceted concept combining three elements: the desire for an outcome, belief in its possibility, and an implicit call to action.[1]

Hope in Today's World

In today's turbulent landscape, hope isn't just a feel-good concept—it's a vital force that enables organizations to endure and thrive. My years working with leaders and organizations have shown me the vital role hope plays during periods of crisis and uncertainty.

Today's workforce faces unprecedented challenges. Employees navigate a complex web of stressors: information overload, global conflicts, economic instability, political division, climate change, and social unrest. These challenges can breed anxiety, cynicism, pessimism, paralysis, and burnout.

The impact of these factors is evident in the data: only 23% of employees are engaged at work, with 15% actively disengaged. Low engagement costs are estimated at US$8.8 trillion or 9% of global GDP. A mere 34% of employees are thriving, whereas 58% struggle and 8% suffer in their work lives. Nearly two-thirds experience anxiety and depression symptoms. Employee stress is at a record high. Almost 40% face negative workplace stress, primarily from workload, lack of control, insufficient support, and leadership issues.[2]

Hope, therefore, is a powerful psychological and emotional resource for individuals, organizations, and communities. It serves as an antidote to paralysis—energizing people to take action rather than retreat into a passive, defensive state. Hope strengthens our ability to handle stress and adversity while providing direction and inspiration. It fuels personal growth and enhances mental health, well-being, and resilience. Beyond individual benefits, hope encourages investment in our collective future, builds community bonds, unites people during difficult times, and sparks shared action.

Hope-Based Leadership

"Leaders are merchants of hope," Napoleon Bonaparte once said.[3] Indeed, leaders profoundly shape employee well-being and engagement—Gallup research shows that managers account for 70% of the variance in team

---

[1] https://plato.stanford.edu/entries/hope/.
[2] https://www.gallup.com/workplace/349484/state-of-the-global-workplace.aspx.
[3] Napoleon I (1916/1769–1821). *Napoleon in His Own Words from the French of Jules Bertaut.* Trans. Herbert Edward Law and Charles Lincoln Rhodes. Chicago, IL: A. C. McClurg & Co.

engagement.[4] In today's complex and rapidly evolving business environment, nurturing and sustaining hope has become essential to effective leadership. Leaders would be wise to recognize their profound influence on their people's well-being.

Hope serves as a beacon, guiding employees through uncertainty. However, while organizations foster hope by establishing clear objectives, success often requires flexibility in pursuing multiple routes to achievement. People need the autonomy to pivot when conditions shift; this adaptability depends on empowerment. Effective leaders actively empower their teams, celebrating achievements to reinforce a sense of agency, confidence, and a hopeful mindset for the future.

Leadership is an emotional journey. It is a great responsibility to lead others to create something. Leaders inspire the people around them to act—if leaders lose hope, energy and momentum dissipate. We all have our fair share of challenges, especially in these turbulent times. Leaders may pretend otherwise, but like everyone else, they can be plagued with doubt, insecurities, and emotional overwhelm. Sometimes, these emotions boil over, creating unpredictable results.

Our choices should reflect our hopes rather than our fears. Hope is grounded in emotional and intellectual honesty. The aim isn't to hope blindly but to balance optimism with realism. This requires personal vulnerability—leaders willing to acknowledge their doubts. Without such honesty, hope can falter, isolating individuals in their worries.

To guide their teams effectively, leaders need emotional literacy—a foundation of self-awareness and self-knowledge that enables them to process their feelings and reflect deeply on their actions. This emotional awareness extends to their teams. By creating space for team members to voice their concerns, leaders serve as emotional anchors, helping to mitigate potentially destructive defensive reactions fueled by anxiety, fear, or anger. Through this vital containment role, leaders can cultivate a constructive environment where individuals and organizations can thrive.

---

[4] https://www.gallup.com/workplace/266822/engaged-employees-differently.aspx#:~:text=With%20leadership%20support%2C%20management%20must,with%20the%20relationships%20they%20establish.

Why This Concern for Reflective Leaders?

My father was born during World War II, when his native Netherlands was under Nazi occupation. These childhood experiences witnessing the impact of destructive leaders, shaped his life's mission: understanding what drives leaders and helping them develop to influence the world positively.

As an economist, psychoanalyst, executive coach, consultant, and management scholar, he has devoted more than five decades to teaching, coaching, and advising leaders. Driven by intellectual curiosity, he has developed various conceptual frameworks to help leaders gain greater insight into their behavior. In his work he weaves between teaching, challenging, nurturing, questioning, and humor as he seeks the most effective approach to help them become unstuck and find more effective ways to lead their organizations. His interventions have transformed the lives of countless leaders. The great hope is that, in turn, these leaders have shaped more human-centered organizations.

Developing Leadership and Change Practitioners

Over the years, my parents and their colleagues have taught several generations of change agents—coaches, consultants, and HR executives. To support these practitioners, they developed a comprehensive toolkit: theoretical models, practical exercises, simulations, and 360-degree feedback instruments. Their work led to the founding of the INSEAD Global Leadership Centre, where they pioneered the integration of coaching—especially group and team approaches—into executive education. Their methods have since become integral to INSEAD's programs and have influenced coaching practices at academic institutions and consulting firms worldwide.

In 2010, my parents founded the Kets de Vries Institute (KDVI) to apply coaching and consulting methodologies in the "real life" context of leaders, teams, and organizations. KDVI's entrepreneurial roots and approach were incubated within two critical INSEAD programs. The first, "The Challenge of Leadership," was created to help top executives deepen their self-awareness and understanding of organizational dynamics. The second, the "Executive Master of Coaching and Consulting for Change" (now "Executive Master in Change"), was created to equip change agents—HR professionals, learning specialists, and team leaders—with the tools to address the human dynamics of organizational transformation. These programs laid the foundation for KDVI's distinctive approach to leadership and organizational change.

The Kets de Vries Institute (KDVI)

As managing director of KDVI, I have assembled teams who can translate the academic leadership research and conceptual work of my parents into practical solutions within the messy arena of real organizational life. The Institute's goal is to have a tangible impact on awareness, mental health, work engagement, group dynamics, and organizational success. We aim to make a small contribution to society by creating places of work that make people feel alive and perform to their very best.[5]

While many organizations struggle to create positive environments, we believe that work can be a profound source of joy and meaning. We've observed that genuine engagement, ownership, energy, and resilience flourish when key elements align:

- Executives have the freedom to tap into their interests and creativity, finding renewed energy and a sense of "flow"[6]
- Executives' values align with those of the organization
- Executives have colleagues who they respect and with whom they feel connected
- Executives feel that they have agency and can speak up and have "voice"
- Executives are part of a learning organization
- Executives know the purpose of their work and see that it makes a difference.

The Profile of Our Consultants

KDVI's practitioners bring a distinctive approach to coaching and consulting. We examine both conscious and unconscious dynamics that shape teams and organizational culture. We develop reflective leaders who understand how unconscious behavior can lead to personal and organizational derailment. By addressing "the elephant in the room"—those issues often left unspoken—we help executives understand deeper behavioral patterns. We guide them to recognize the "scripts" in their own "inner theater" and that of others, enabling them to motivate teams more effectively and create organizations where people excel.

---

[5] Manfred F. R. Kets de Vries (2001). "Creating Authentizotic Organizations: Well-Functioning Individuals in Vibrant Companies." *Human Relations*, 54(1):101–111.
[6] Mihaly Csikszentmihalyi (2022). *Flow: The Psychology of Happiness*. London: Rider.

Although we love to do proactive work, KDVI often helps leaders in times of transition and difficulty, when choices are hard and complex and there is a lack of clarity and direction. For them, we create safe spaces and the time to reflect, increase their awareness, learn, manage emotions, and reframe. Leaders cannot always turn to their teams for this support—sometimes, they need an unbiased party with whom they can explore situations with new eyes.

Finding the right coaching partner for senior leaders (Board/Exco) requires careful consideration. The foundation is building trust and an effective working alliance. Therefore, KDVI associates must possess exceptional emotional literacy, sharp diagnostic skills, the confidence to speak truth to power, and be subtle and adept enough to be heard when they do. This is why we work with seasoned practitioners who have established their own successful practices. Also, they are anything but "hungry" consultants. Our consultants aren't into the creation of dependency relationships—instead, they focus on empowering clients to stand on their own two feet.

A Personal Note

Given the behavior of many political leaders today, my parents and team members are deeply troubled by the state of our world. Often, it seems humanity has no learning curve—all too quickly, we fall into primitive defensive reactions. Many current signs echo the difficult times my father was born into and has worked so hard to prevent from recurring.

As Erich Fromm, the German American psychoanalyst and humanistic philosopher noted, "What holds true for the individual holds true for a society. It is never static; if it does not grow, it decays; if it does not transcend the status quo for the better, it changes for the worse."[7] While the media often presents a doomsday narrative, we should not just let it be. What we need instead is a balanced and hopeful vision of the future. This requires emotionally intelligent leaders who can guide us through complexity while maintaining both realism and optimism. This book offers practical tools and insights for developing such reflective leaders—the kind of leaders our world

---

[7] Erich Fromm (2010). *The Revolution of Hope: Towards a Humanized Technology.* New York: American Mental Health Foundation.

desperately needs to be able to navigate current challenges, to shape a better tomorrow.

Oriane Kets de Vries
Managing Director, KDVI

Preface

The Two Snakes

There was once a snake that lived at the bottom of a dark, dried-out well. The well was the only world the snake knew and life, though limited, was good. Small creatures regularly fell into the well providing him with food, and he lived content and secure in his deep, dank world.

One day, a snake that lived in a nearby field passed by the well and looked down. The snake living in the well was excited at this unexpected new company and welcomed him. They talked freely—the snake in the well boasting of his good fortune, his safe, quiet life, and reliable food.

The field snake listened carefully to all his new companion said before telling him of the vast opportunities available to snakes such as himself. He described a world of large forests and meadows, of open skies and a far wider array of creatures to eat.

The snake of the well promptly dismissed all the other snake had to say, convinced that his well was the best and the safest place to live—why would he ever wish to change it?

The field snake was persistent though, encouraging the well snake to see for himself what the world had to offer, but the well snake merely shook his head, fearful of the unknown, of leaving behind his comfort for a life full of potential dangers.

Disappointed, the field snake slithered away, continuing his exploits in the great wide world. He was adventurous, he embraced every new challenge he encountered on his travels, and had led a long, interesting, and satisfactory life. The well snake wasn't as fortunate—soon after his encounter with the field snake, a thunderstorm struck and its torrential rains filled the well in a flash, drowning him.

A Tale of Change

A tale such as this one, though about snakes, has parallels in the lives of people, especially as I reflect on the many leaders and organizations we have supported as leadership coaches and consultants. This tale, after all, is one with a moral: changing behavior is neither a simple nor a comfortable process. Change can be hard and, for many people, "unlearning" habitual patterns is an uphill challenge. Think about how difficult it is for most of us to keep our New Year's resolutions. More often than not our resolutions don't lead anywhere, and it is estimated that 70% of significant change initiatives fail. Clearly, this is not a statistic readily volunteered by consultants and executive coaches. More commonly they make outsized claims of their successes in changing people and organizations when the reality is quite different.

> *Changing behavior is neither a simple nor a comfortable process.*

In our work as consultants and coaches, we have a more realistic outlook. Inevitably we have had our failures; however, through trial and error, we have created an intervention methodology that has proved successful in helping people and organizations change. Now, in this book, we wish to share some of our methods and observations concerning change management. Here, we demonstrate—while paying attention to the psychological, individual, and organizational dynamics that are at play—how change methodologies can be applied in a highly effective way. We hope that our contributions will be helpful to professional trainers, consultants, executive coaches, educators, academics, and managers in becoming more effective change agents. Implementing such strategies may mean they no longer have to kick the can down the road. In addition, to make the chapters more readable, we aren't referencing throughout the book. There will, however, be a comprehensive bibliography at the end.

> *Life stops for no one—every moment is transient, every situation impermanent.*

Change will always be painful, but not as painful as remaining stuck. As the story of the two snakes illustrates, we can't change our lives without stepping out of our comfort zones. In fact, change often only begins at the extremities of our comfort zones and the steps required can be quite disturbing. However, if we don't change, we don't grow. And if we don't grow, we aren't really living. We must remember that life stops for no one—every moment is transient, every situation impermanent. In the wise words of British politician Harold Wilson, "the secret of change is to focus all of your energy not on fighting the old, but on building the new."[1]

Manfred F. R. Kets de Vries
Paris, France

---

[1] Harold Wilson (1967). Speech to the Consultative Assembly of the Council of Europe, Strasbourg, France (January 23, 1967); reported in *The New York Times* (January 24, 1967), p. 12.

Contents

Foreword		v
Preface		xiii
Contents		xvii
List of Figures		xxi
About the Author		xxiii
1	**Introduction**	1
	What Do We Mean by "C" and "I" Organizations?	2
	Being Clinical	4
2	**The Clinical Paradigm**	7
	Being at the "Bedside"	8
	Freudian Origins	8
	A Systemic Perspective	10
	Other Conceptual Frameworks	12
	A Psychodynamic-Systemic Focus	15
3	**Human Dilemmas in Leadership**	17
	The Narcissistic Temptation	18
	Change Resistances	20
	The EQ Factor	23

		Finding the Leader Within	24
		The Reinvention Process	25
4	**Socio-dynamics**		27
		The Psychodynamics of Groups	28
		Social Defense Mechanisms	30
		Folie à deux	30
5	**The Coaching Conundrum**		33
		What Is Executive Coaching All About?	34
		Splitters and Bundlers	35
		Internal Versus External	37
		The Objectives of Individual Coaching	37
		Moving with the Resistances	39
6	**Teams and Company**		41
		How Effective Are Teams?	42
		Team Dysfunctionality	45
		Leadership Group (Team) Coaching Comes to the Rescue	47
		The Trust Equation	47
		Creating "Aha" Experiences	48
		Catalysts of Change	49
7	**The Leadership Audit**		53
		The Instrumentation	54
		Being Surrounded by Liars	57
		Creating an Effective Scenario	58
		With Unity Comes Strength	61
8	**The Three Mental Triangles**		63
		The Triangle of Mental Life	64
		The Triangle of Conflict	66
		The Triangle of Relationships	68
		Linking the Past with the Present	70
		Restructuring a Person's Inner Theater	72
9	**Deconstructing the Individual Change Process**		79
		Banging Your Head Against a Brick Wall	81
		The Stages of Individual Change	82
		Prerequisites of Personal Change	83
		Step 1: Negative Emotions	83
		Step 2: The Focal Event	85

	Step 3: The "Public" Declaration of Intent	86
	Step 4: The Inner Journey	87
	Step 5: The Internalization of Change	87
10	**Creating a Transitional Space**	89
	Reframing and Encouragement	90
	The Challenge of Transcendence	91
	Actively Working on the Problem	91
	The Group as Projective Screen	92
	Listening with the Third Ear	93
	Consolidating the Change	96
	What Does a Positive Outcome Entail?	97
11	**Navigating the Maze of Organizational Transformation**	99
	The Organizational Change Journey	101
	Creating Dissatisfaction	101
	Engendering Hope	102
	Carrying out the Transformation	105
	Staging Transformative Events	106
	Transforming the Past	111
12	**The Process of Letting Go**	115
	Letting Go	116
	Additional Factors Facilitating Change	118
	Social Support	118
	Locus of Control	120
	The Hardiness Factor	121
13	**The Holistic Picture: Culture and Organization**	123
	Influencing an Organization's Culture	125
	Toward a Coaching Culture: A Case Example	126
	Bottom-Up and Top-Down	129
	The Objectives of Organizational Coaching	131
	A Socratic Method of Leadership Coaching	134
	Assessing the Effectiveness of the Interventions	137
14	**The Senior Executive "Recycling" Workshops**	139
	Open Enrollment	140
	A Bird's Eye View	142
	A Personal Interlude	145
	Taking the Road Less Traveled	147
	A Case Example	149
	The Drivers of Change Revisited	150

15 Major Life Themes — 153
The Haunting Questions — 154
  Loss — 154
  Interpersonal Conflict — 155
  Boredom — 156
  Addictions — 156
  Developmental Imbalance — 157
  Life Balance — 158
  The Primacy of Meaning — 158
  The Stealth Motivator — 159

16 The Authentizotic Puzzle — 163
Best Place to Work — 164
The Authentizotic Organization Checklist — 168
Staying Out of the Wormhole — 169

17 Love and Work — 171
The "Healthy" Individual — 172
Motivational Need Systems — 174
Finding Meaning in Life — 178
  Meaning in Life Questionnaire — 180
Developing Reflective People — 181
Making the Best of a Poor Hand of Cards — 184

Epigraph Sources — 187

Recommended Readings — 193

Index — 199

List of Figures

Fig. 2.1	Conceptual models facilitating individual & organizational change	15
Fig. 8.1	Triangle of Mental Life	65
Fig. 8.2	Triangle of Conflict	66
Fig. 8.3	Triangle of Relationships	69
Fig. 8.4	The Three Triangles of Insight	72
Fig. 9.1	Individual stages of change	88
Fig. 11.1	The corporate transformation process	107
Fig. 11.2	The assessment process	109
Fig. 17.1	Our existential challenges	181
Fig. 17.2	Meaning in Life Questionnaire	182

About the Author

Manfred F. R. Kets de Vries brings a different view to the much-studied subjects of psychotherapy, organizational dynamics, leadership, executive coaching, consulting, and psychotherapy. Bringing to bear his knowledge and experience of economics (Econ. Drs., University of Amsterdam), management (ITP, MBA, and DBA, Harvard Business School), and psychoanalysis (Membership Canadian Psychoanalytic Society, Paris Psychoanalytic Society, and the International Psychoanalytic Association), he explores individual, organizational, and societal existential dilemmas in depth.

The Distinguished Clinical Professor of Leadership Development and Organizational Change at INSEAD, he is the Founder of INSEAD's Executive Master Program in Change Management and has been the founder/director of INSEAD's Global Leadership Centre. He has been a pioneer in team coaching as an intervention method to help organizations and people change. As an educator, Professor Kets de Vries has received INSEAD's distinguished MBA teacher award six times. He has held professorships at McGill University, the École des Hautes Études Commerciales, Montreal, and the Harvard Business School. He is also a distinguished visiting professor at the European School for Management and Technology (ESMT), Berlin and has lectured at management institutions around the world. *The Financial Times*, *Le Capital*, *Wirtschaftswoche*, and *The Economist* have rated Kets de

Vries among the world's leading management thinkers and one of the most influential contributors to human resource management.

Professor Kets de Vries is the author, co-author, or editor of almost 60 books, including *The Neurotic Organization*; *Power and the Corporate Mind*; *Organizational Paradoxes*; *Struggling with the Demon: Perspectives on Individual and Organizational Irrationality*; *Handbook of Character Studies*; *The Irrational Executive*; *Leaders, Fools and Impostors*; *Life and Death in the Executive Fast Lane*; *Prisoners of Leadership*; *The Leadership Mystique*; *The Happiness Equation*; *Are Leaders Born or Are They Made? The Case of Alexander the Great*; *The New Russian Business Elite*; *Leadership by Terror: Finding Shaka Zulu in the Attic*; *The Leader on the Couch*; *Coach and Couch*; *The Family Business on the Couch*; *Sex, Money, Happiness, and Death: The Quest for Authenticity*; *Reflections on Leadership and Character*; *Reflections on Leadership and Career*; *Reflections on Organizations*; *The Coaching Kaleidoscope*; *The Hedgehog Effect: The Secrets of High Performance Teams*; *Mindful Leadership Coaching: Journeys into the Interior*; *You Will Meet a Tall Dark Stranger: Executive Coaching Challenges*; *Telling Fairy Tales in the Boardroom: How to Make Sure Your Organization Lives Happily Ever After*; *Riding the Leadership Roller Coaster: A Psychological Observer's Guide*; *Down the Rabbit Hole of Leadership: Leadership Pathology of Everyday Life*; *The CEO Whisperer: Meditations on Leadership, Life and Change*; *Quo Vadis: The Existential Challenges of Leaders*; *Leadership Unhinged: Essays on the Ugly, the Bad, and the Weird*; *Leading Wisely: Becoming a Reflective Leader in Turbulent Times*; *The Daily Perils of Executive Life: How to Survive When Dancing on Quicksand*; *The Path to Authentic Leadership: Dancing with the Ouroboros*; *A Life Well Lived: Dialogues with a Kabouter*; and *The Darker Side of Leadership: Pythons Devouring Crocodiles*; *Storytelling for Leaders: Tales of Sorrow and Love*; and *Narcissistic Leadership: Narcissus on the Couch*. Furthermore, he has designed a number of 360-degree feedback instruments, including the widely used *Global Executive Leadership Mirror*, *Global Executive Leadership Inventory*, *Leadership Archetype Questionnaire*, and the *Organizational Culture Audit*.

In addition, Kets de Vries has published more than 400 academic papers as chapters in books and as articles. He has also written more than 100 case studies, including seven that received the Best Case of the Year award. He has written hundreds of mini-articles (blogs) for the *Harvard Business Review*, *INSEAD Knowledge*, and other digital outlets. He is also a regular writer for various other magazines. His work has been featured in such publications as *The New York Times*, *The Wall Street Journal*, *The Los Angeles Times*, *Fortune*, *Business Week*, *The Economist*, *The Financial Times*, *The Straits Times*, *The New*

Statesman, The Harvard Business Review, Le Figaro, El Pais, and *Het Financieele Dagblad*. His books and articles have been translated into more than 30 languages.

Professor Kets de Vries is a member of 17 editorial boards and is a Fellow of the Academy of Management. He is on the board of various charitable organizations and is also a founding member of the International Society for the Psychoanalytic Study of Organizations (ISPSO), which has honored him as a lifetime member. Kets de Vries is also the first non-US recipient of the International Leadership Association Lifetime Achievement Award for his contributions to leadership research and development. He has received a Lifetime Achievement Award from Germany for his advancement of executive education. The American Psychological Association has honored him with the "Harry and Miriam Levinson Award" for his contributions to Organizational Consultation. For his work to further the interface between management and psychoanalysis, Professor Kets de Vries is the recipient of the "Freud Memorial Award". He has also received the "Vision of Excellence Award" from the Harvard Institute of Coaching. Kets de Vries is the first beneficiary of INSEAD's Dominique Héau Award for "Inspiring Educational Excellence." Furthermore, he has been honored with four honorary doctorates. The Dutch government has made him an Officer in the Order of Oranje Nassau.

Kets de Vries works as a consultant on organizational design/transformation and strategic human resource management for companies worldwide. He has worked with companies such as McKinsey, Bain, Goldman Sachs, Standard Bank of South Africa, South African Breweries, National Australian Bank, Heineken, ABN/AMRO, Air Liquide, Schlumberger, and others. As an educator and consultant, he has worked in more than 40 countries. In his role as a consultant, he is also the founder-chairman of the Kets de Vries Institute (KDVI)—a boutique global strategic leadership development consulting firm with associates worldwide (www.kdvi.com).

On a personal note, Kets de Vries was the first fly fisherman in Outer Mongolia (at the time becoming the world record holder of the Siberian *hucho taimen* trout). He is a member of New York's Explorers Club and in his spare time he can be found in the rainforests or savannas of Central and Southern Africa, the Siberian taiga, the Ussuri Krai, Kamchatka, the Pamir Mountain Range, the Altai Mountains, Arnhem Land, or within the Arctic Circle.

E-mail: manfred.ketsdevries@insead.edu
Website: www.kdvi.com

1

Introduction

Things and actions are what they are, and the consequences of them will be what they will be: why, then, should we desire to be deceived?
—Joseph Butler

He that is come to the top of wisdom and practice, spends every day as if it were his last, and is never guilty of over-excitement, sluggishness, or insincerity.
—Marcus Aurelius

"I do not deny," said Don Quixote, "that what happened to us may be worth laughing at, but it is not worth making a story about, for it is not everyone that is shrewd enough to hit the right point of a thing."
—Miguel de Cervantes

Recollections of a Younger Self

While talking about our interest in change management during a visit to Goa, one individual offered an insightful recollection of his younger self:

> "When I was young, I would ask myself, 'Give me the energy so that I can change the whole world.' I saw so many things that I thought were very wrong. I was relatively immature and impatient then, and I wanted to change the face of the Earth.
>
> But as I grew a little older, I began to think: 'This seems too difficult—almost half of my life has passed and still I haven't changed a single person.' I began to feel the whole world was too large to deal

with, and so I turned instead to my family, thinking 'let me at least try to change them.'

As I became older still, I realized that even trying to change my family might be too much. Who am I to change them anyway? I came to see that to change myself would be more than enough, and to accomplish any change, I needed to start with myself."

What Do We Mean by "C" and "I" Organizations?

We live in an age of rapid, unrelenting change. The traditional organizations of the past, built by increments, have all but disappeared. For many, the resulting uncertainties have triggered distress, trepidation, fear, anxiety, and resistance. In addition to such individual disquiet is the way that organizations have become progressively more complex. "C" organizations have been replaced by "I" organizations. By this we mean those organizations driven by a traditional **C**ommand, **C**ontrol, and **C**ompartmentalization mentality ("C" organizations) have declined, giving way to those constructed through **I**nteraction, **I**nformation, and **I**nnovation (the "I" organizations). In this new digital world, tall organizations are out whereas flatter organizations flourish—a transformation that requires people to be more adept at networking. Such sizeable changes have exerted far greater pressures on executives and their people to manage the paradoxes intrinsic to organizational life, and to do so rapidly.

Since, in these networked "I" organizations more work must occur in a team setting, it has become increasingly important to adapt to the needs of employees. As a result, those who lead organizations have to be highly attuned to the needs of the people they're dealing with; emotional intelligence becomes paramount. The ability to adapt successfully to other people's needs and desires has become sine qua non. For those leaders who are able to do so, the sky is the limit.

> *At the heart of effective organizations lies human action—what we do, how we do it, and why we do it.*

At the heart of effective organizations lies human action—what we do, how we do it, and why we do it. Therefore, close attention has to be paid to the organizational setting, including individual and group dynamics. We have learned that in order to be successful, those in leadership positions must be highly aware and empathic of the inevitable anxieties that are part and parcel of human life, and to get the best out of their people they need to address these concerns head-on.

In high-performance organizations, we can see how leaders harness human energy and inspire their people toward constructive action. We strongly believe that the people who run organizations need to utilize and leverage the diverse and complex psychological dynamics of organizational life in order to succeed. Leaders must recognize the importance of what have been referred to as "the soft skills," essentially using emotional intelligence to their advantage. Contrary to their name, these abilities are often the "hardest" skills to learn.

> *Contrary to their name, the "soft skills" of leadership are often the hardest to learn.*

By recognizing the importance of emotional life in organizations, the people who lead them have to appreciate that all their actions and activities must attend to both conscious and unconscious processes. In fact, most of our behavior is unconsciously driven and highly influential on the way we behave and the actions we take, perhaps even to a greater extent than the more conscious processes.

For many people, the suggestion that they may not be in control of their behavior is hard to accept. Most of our actions tend to be multi-layered—the expression "whenever people talk about the weather, in reality, they are talking about something else," says it all. Thus, whatever we do, these many layers need to be taken into consideration.

> *For many people, the suggestion that they may not be in control of their behavior is hard to accept.*

Historically, it can be seen that people interested in organizational processes are dubious about venturing into the emotional and psychological realm of organizational life. They fear its messy, real-life complexities and subsequently limit their focus to the more rational side of human behavior. Understanding the reasons why people behave "irrationally" simply isn't "their cup of tea." However, this oversimplified approach to human behavior means any change efforts they implement have been of a quick-fix, superficial nature that pay little or no attention to the more deep-seated underlying processes.

This outlook on leadership and organizations will only ever be skin deep, and most interventions will be devoid of enduring influence. The result is that many puzzling organizational phenomena remain unresolved and unexplained. Most often, no attention is given to the elephant in the room, the controversial issues that are obviously present but are avoided as a subject of discussion.

Given all we know about change management, we thus suggest that any meaningful investigation of human behavior must have a rational component and an irrational component. This necessitates looking more deeply into the world of work with the aim of untangling and explaining what lies below the surface. We need to see through the darkness that may lead us astray, yet this kind of "night vision"—to make the irrational more rational—requires in-depth observation. To find out what is really happening demands a more "clinical orientation."

> *Any meaningful investigation of human behavior must have a rational component and an irrational component.*

Being Clinical

So, what do we mean by "clinical"? The word itself is derived from the Greek *klinike*, referring to the action of physicians visiting patients at their sickbeds. Those interested in the clinical approach aren't dealing in abstract theory but focused action, and their proximity means they are able to see what's really going on. A similar process is necessary if we are serious about wanting to understand organizational life. We need to take on the role of clinician and look deeply into the prevailing psychological dynamics.

> *If we are serious about wanting to understand organizational life, we need to take on the role of clinician and look deeply into the prevailing psychological dynamics.*

People interested in change management will be more effective if they pay greater attention to the underlying motives that govern people's behavior. Naturally, this process requires that those in leadership positions play a primary role and hence their behavior needs to be the first that is put under the microscope. We need to understand *why* they do what they do and assess what makes them effective, as much as what makes them ineffective. Contrary to the writings of the many management theorists who attribute leadership effectiveness to mere environmental constraints or structural factors, we believe it is important to recognize that the psychological dynamics between leaders and followers has a significant influence on what's going on and must be taken into consideration if we are to make sense of organizational life. This does not discount the context in which leaders operate, yet recognizes an organization can have all the "environmental" advantages in the world—strong financial resources, enviable market position, and state-of-the-art technology—but still fail. This can often be due to an overreliance on structural models that distract from or obscure the importance of the "bedside" clinical observation.

What differentiates our strategy from more traditional consultants and coaches is our emphasis on this clinical approach to leadership and organizational studies—the metaphorical "bedside manner" that can be a game changer in successful leadership. Our aim is to comprehend more about the dynamics of organizational life, become more effective change agents, and, ultimately, serve our clients better.

> *People's everyday lives are webs of constantly shifting and irrational forces that underlie seemingly "rational" behaviors and choices.*

Intrinsic to our method is the acknowledgment that people's everyday lives are webs of constantly shifting and irrational forces that underlie seemingly "rational" behaviors and choices—and that includes life in the workplace. In the work we do, we are always cognizant of the fact that leaders and the people who they lead, like the rest of us, will not be paragons of rationality. Seemingly irrational behavioral patterns will be more the rule than the exception. By acknowledging the underlying causes of apparent irrationality, we can understand more about why so many well-laid plans and strategies derail or, conversely, why otherwise effective leaders sometimes act in unexpected ways. As change agents, we never forget that organizational leaders, and their workforces, are not one-dimensional entities, but complex and paradoxical individuals who radiate diverse emotions from soaring idealism to gloomy pessimism; they may show stubborn short-sightedness, courageous vision, narrow-minded suspicion, and open-handed trust, or be driven by irrational envy, greed, and unbelievable selfishness. Being willing, open, and cognizant of these underlying psychological dynamics of human behavior has led us to a more realistic view of life in organizations. By applying the clinical approach to the ebb and flow of life we establish a deeper understanding of the vicissitudes in organizational and leadership behavior. Through investing time in making sense of people's latent wishes and fantasies and tracing how these influence behavior in the organizational world—applying the clinical paradigm to our interventions—we can ascertain how leaders and organizations really function. Though they may appear strange at times, our methods adopt a highly pragmatic perspective in order to solve seemingly knotty organizational problems.

> *Organizational leaders, and their workforces, are not one-dimensional entities, but complex and paradoxical individuals who radiate diverse emotions from soaring idealism to gloomy pessimism.*

2

The Clinical Paradigm

*The last of sights, the last of days; and no man's life account as gain
Ere the full tale be finished and the darkness find him without pain.*
—Sophocles

The physician must be able to tell the antecedents, know the present, and foretell the future—must mediate these things, and have two special objects in view with regard to disease, namely, to do good or to do no harm.
—Hippocrates

Illness is the doctor to whom we pay most heed; to kindness, to knowledge, we make promises only; pain we obey.
—Marcel Proust

The Nobleman and the Zen Master

A nobleman visited a Zen master and told him that he wished to be enlightened. The Zen master asked him if he was willing to undergo all the challenges that come with enlightenment, to which the nobleman answered affirmatively. Immediately afterwards, the Zen master asked the nobleman what he was good at and he replied that he was an excellent chess player. With this knowledge, the Zen master arranged a game between the nobleman and a monk who was a beginner at chess. He explained to the nobleman that the rule of the game was that whoever lost would be beheaded.

Inevitably the nobleman was much better at the game, but all the while he was winning, he struggled with his conscience: on the one hand he wanted to become enlightened, but in the process, he might cause the poor monk's death. With this predicament in mind the nobleman began to play badly. Yet, whereas playing well came easily to him, playing badly without being obvious was a surprisingly difficult task, requiring considerable ingenuity. The nobleman played on at the edge of his nerves, sweating profusely, until the Zen master eventually stopped the game and said to him: "Your first lesson is over. You have learned a number of things today: empathy, compassion, concentration, and resilience. Express your gratefulness to your chess opponent for making it possible."

Being at the "Bedside"

The "clinical" approach draws on ideas from psychoanalysis (in particular, object relations theory), dynamic psychotherapy, developmental psychology, family systems theory, paradoxical intervention, motivational interviewing, neuroscience, evolutionary psychology, group dynamics, and cognitive theories. The umbrella term "clinical paradigm" has been taken to summarize the practical application of many of these theories within an organizational setting.

Freudian Origins

The term "clinical paradigm" derives from the psychoanalytical theories of human behavior proposed by Sigmund Freud. Specifically, this approach draws attention to the sources of energy and motivational forces that drive human actions by considering what is "within"—the inner world of individuals, including their emotions—and relationships between individuals—the "reality" created by the dynamics of groups. Although Freud himself did not make any specific directions about the application of his ideas to the world of work, the psychoanalytically oriented clinical paradigm was taken up by many of his contemporaries and became a conceptual framework for the analysis of social phenomena. Many social scientists influenced by Freud's contributions applied aspects of the clinical paradigm to the workplace by claiming that the inner world of the leader—his or her early childhood experiences and emotions—was a fundamental basis for his or her social behavior in later life.

In the light of progressively more advanced information concerning the workings of the mind, a number of Freudian theories are no longer considered valid. Others, however, after being scientifically and empirically tested and verified, have become the cornerstones of psychoanalytic theory and technique. In this respect, many of Freud's ideas relating to cognitive and emotional processes have retained their relevance, and much of our methodology is grounded in this clinical paradigm. This includes our understanding of the vicissitudes of organizational behavior and the people working in such systems; the hidden dynamics at play and how these can be harnessed for the purpose of individual and organizational growth. Metaphorically speaking, our practice involves placing ourselves at the "bedside" of organizational life.

> *Irrational behavior is commonplace in organizational life, but it nearly always has a rationale to it.*

The clinical paradigm is based on a number of premises:

- *What you see isn't necessarily what you get.* The world around us is much more complex than a superficial view suggests. Much of what happens is beyond conscious awareness.
- *We are not always rational human beings.* Paradoxically, irrationality is grounded in rationality. Irrational behavior is commonplace in organizational life, but it nearly always has a rationale to it. This rationale is critical in understanding a person's inner theater—the core themes that affect an individual's personality and their subsequent leadership style. Well-intentioned and well-thought-out plans are derailed daily in offices around the world as a result of psychological dynamics and forces that are beyond consciousness. Finding this rationale is rarely easy, however in our approach we adopt the Sherlock Holmes of corporate life—the organizational detective adept at teasing out what's really going on beneath an executive's quirky behavior or an employee's questionable attitudes.
- *We are subjected to various motivational need systems.* These determine our character and create the tightly interlocked triangle of our mental life (the three points of which are cognition, emotions, and behavior). In order to influence behavioral patterns, both cognition and emotions need to be taken into consideration. Emotions determine many of our actions and an understanding of them plays a vital role in effective leadership; put simply, emotional intelligence is a necessity.
- *We all have a dark side.* However much leaders may be depicted as paragons of virtue with all the glowing attributes their role demands,

all leaders—and indeed all people—have a darker side. Many leaders are derailed by the blind spots in their personality that they (or we) have failed to recognize.

> *We are a product of our past. ... We tend to repeat, replicate, and respond to certain behavioral patterns that, like it or not, demonstrate a continuity between past and present.*

- *We are a product of our past.* As the saying goes, the hand that rocks the cradle rules the world. Ultimately, the way we behave is the result not just of our genetic endowment but also the developmental circumstances of our early years. We tend to repeat, replicate, and respond to certain behavioral patterns that, like it or not, demonstrate a continuity between past and present.

In our work as executive coaches we have ascertained that the application of this clinical paradigm is a valuable tool in teasing out and addressing the human dilemmas of leadership. It has helped us to explore the roles that leaders, both consciously and unconsciously, have cast themselves in, and assisted us in identifying self-defeating expectations, negative self-appraisals, and outdated perceptions—behavioral patterns that may once have served a useful purpose but have later proved counterproductive. The structure of the clinical paradigm has also provided a way to illuminate the psychological processes that occur in teams. Here, it has been an effective way of ascertaining the complementary qualities, dynamics, and positioning of those in executive roles. Moreover, it has been instrumental in gaining a more objective understanding of an organization's culture with its prevailing systems, structures, and strategies.

A Systemic Perspective

Psychoanalytic psychology has been instrumental to our work. However, aspects of systems theory also form an essential component of our clinical paradigm. An understanding of systems theory provides a valuable way of interpreting the group dynamics that are intrinsic to organizations—the systems of behaviors and psychological processes that act within a social group (intragroup dynamics) or between social groups (intergroup dynamics).

Systems theory is an interdisciplinary theory concerning the way complex systems operate in nature, society, and science. It is a framework by which we can investigate and/or describe any group of objects that work together to produce a specific result. The theoretical basis of this systemic orientation is to view people in relation to each other rather than to focus mainly or exclusively on what is happening within the individual.

> *Systems theory is a framework by which we can investigate and/or describe any group of objects that work together to produce a specific result.*

Effectively, the systemic perspective acknowledges that people do not exist in isolation from one another, but rather as part of interconnected units. Although its origins are in biology, it has also proved helpful in explaining the behavior of people within organizations. Systems theory deals fundamentally with relationships, offering insights about the interactions, patterns, and dynamics within groups.

To adopt a systemic approach, a focus is placed on the complex network of relationships in which people function, their social context, and the problems that may arise as a result of group dynamics. This outlook has helped us to discern specific patterns of behavior, identify how they came to be established, and their implications for different group members. This mode of systemic observation has only highlighted what we already know of the connections between intrapsychic and interpersonal perspectives in relation to individuals, couples, families, teams, and organizations and this learning has enabled us to explore particular patterns of belief and behavioral roles that have become set over time. Understanding why people are stuck is key to enabling them to decide when change is desirable or necessary. Lastly, applying systemic theories has allowed us to explore more deeply not only how people communicate, but also *what* they communicate.

> *Understanding why people are stuck is key to enabling them to decide when change is desirable or necessary.*

Other Conceptual Frameworks

In our pursuit to gain a better understanding of people and organizations, we appreciate the value of moving seamlessly from an individual to a systemic orientation. Our effectiveness as "organizational clinicians," however, has been enriched by familiarity with other models of individual and organizational change. In fact, we would go as far as to say that something of our success as change agents owes much to the eclectic use of a number of conceptual frameworks, and a willingness to adapt them to the diverse situations that are presented to us. Therefore, as noted, in addition to the more psychodynamic-systemic orientation, we regularly refer to a number of other conceptual schemes to help leverage meaningful change.

An example of this would be the application of ideas derived from **short-term dynamic psychotherapy**. In this form of intervention we, as "clinicians," try to solve problematic issues within the shortest possible timeframe. Short-term dynamic psychotherapy involves looking at the most essential patterns in interpersonal dynamics under the lens of various mental triangles that influence human behavior (this is explored further in Chapter 8). Features that are characteristic of this kind of intervention method include a focus on affect and emotional expression, self-experience and relatedness, maladaptive relationship patterns, the exploration of unconscious motives and fantasies, and the relating of current experiences to influential past experiences. Much of this approach is influenced by psychoanalytic concepts, however the "dynamic" aspect refers to the exploration of the unconscious as fundamental to the internal struggles people experience in the present.

A **developmental orientation** is another framework fundamental to our practice, by which we mean a consideration of the longer-term process of human growth from the prenatal stage through infancy, childhood, adolescence, and adulthood; this encompasses physical, cognitive, social, intellectual, perceptual, and emotional growth. Unsurprisingly, a significant proportion of theories within this discipline focus on childhood development as the period of an individual's lifespan where the greatest changes occur, and where one achieves many significant physical, emotional, and social milestones.

Further ideas we incorporate in our practice include those of **evolutionary psychology** and the biologically informed study of human behavior. This approach looks at human cognition, emotions, and behavior that are the effects of long-term human evolution. In this respect, evolutionary psychology combines both psychological and biological scientific traditions. Utilizing their conceptual frameworks, it seeks to explain how and why aspects of being human, such as emotions, have, over time, been an advantage to our ancestors. This assumes that certain internal mechanisms are the adaptations and products of natural selection which have helped our ancestors to travel, survive, and reproduce to a greater extent than other species.

Additional insights originate from the field of **neuroscience**, which typically examines the brain's neurotransmissions and the psychological events associated with biological activity. Neuroscience seeks to demonstrate how a social setting can affect our brain circuitry and biochemistry, which are also influenced by genetic controls. In turn, these neurobiological mechanisms will affect behavior, and the proponents of neuroscience hypothesize such brain mechanisms will eventually and exhaustively explain the mind and, in time, human nature itself.

> *All people have the capacity for self-understanding, and yet our unique identity can only be fully understood through our relationships with others.*

Where appropriate, our interventions have also borrowed ideas from **existential psychology**. The reason for this is that our work is inclined toward a holistic consideration of human behavior. We believe in the importance of not only identifying and reducing the symptoms of toxic behavior patterns but also in addressing how a person defines meaning, purpose, and, ultimately, achieves a well-lived life. In this, we are concerned not only with "being" but also with "becoming"; a pursuit founded on the belief that all people have the capacity for self-understanding, and yet our unique identity can only be fully understood through our relationships with others.

At the same time, we recognize that humans continually recreate themselves as a way of adapting to the constantly changing nature of life. Our work is intended to foster each client's pursuit of self-fulfillment by helping them to make authentic, meaningful, and self-directed choices. Thus, our interventions are also aligned toward the necessity for free will, self-determination, and the search for meaning.

Encouraging self-determination is one of the intentions behind our use of **motivational interviewing**—a form of intervention that requires the client to argue for change. It equates to a form of resistance judo and has proven to be a useful concept that encourages an individual to make and consolidate decisions and opinions. This method of interaction is a directive, client-centered counseling style that elicits behavioral change by helping clients explore and resolve their ambivalence about certain actions that they need to take. We have learned the hard way that mandatory approaches to change are not long-term solutions, and so in using this methodology we endeavor to be non-judgmental, non-confrontational, and non-adversarial. By increasing our clients' awareness of what the root causes of their problems may be, they must also address the consequences and potential risks that may result. By the reiteration of their motivations, we try to lead those who may have thought about potential change closer to the steps required to put such change into action.

> We have learned the hard way that mandatory approaches to change are not long-term solutions.

In situations where we encounter serious resistance to change, we have found that a method of ***paradoxical intervention*** can apply some leverage. The intention here is to first and foremost strategically maneuver the client into recognizing the problem and then to understanding how they may have created the problem and the lack of experiential knowledge that perpetuates it. Our greatest challenge is that of altering the self-sustaining nature of a negative behavior or symptom. Paradoxical intervention does this by forcing the client to engage in the opposite behavior, and in doing so interrupts the reinforcing feedback loops that may be maintaining a problem. One of the salient elements of this change-inducing tactic is that of surprise—being forced to engage in an unexpected approach may be the very thing that helps a client out of their comfort zone, from where they may reflect on their specific challenge with fresh eyes. In fact, the client may realize that certain actions they had deemed beyond their control are in fact the result of some unconscious compulsion. By communicating two apparently contradictory messages, for example prescribing the symptom by making the symptom they want to resolve worse, the client may achieve a different frame of reference, a new way of looking at the problem, and the leverage or "tipping point" toward a solution.

> By means of paradoxical intervention, for example by communicating two apparently contradictory messages, ... the client may achieve a different frame of reference, a new way of looking at the problem, and the leverage or "tipping point" towards a solution.

In all forms of intervention, we stress the value of consultants and coaches speaking the language of the people with whom they are working. Change agents are at their most effective when they have a deep understanding of

Conceptual Models Facilitating Individual & Organizational Change

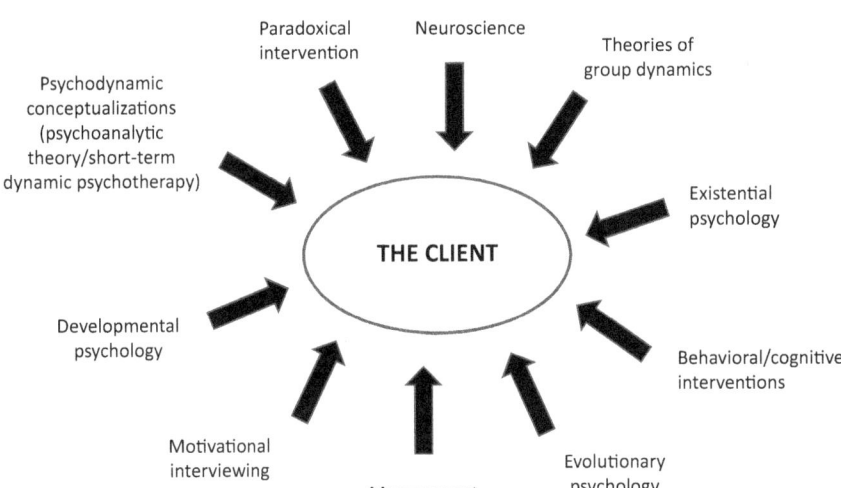

Fig. 2.1 Conceptual models facilitating individual & organizational change

their practice and its management, and therefore the language of management needs to be used when explaining the requisite steps that will be taken to encourage change. (See Fig. 2.1 for a summary of the various conceptual models facilitating individual and organizational change.)

A Psychodynamic-Systemic Focus

This chapter has given an overview of some of the intervention techniques we may utilize in our practice, summarized by using the term of the clinical paradigm. However, our governing clinical approach is that of a psychodynamic-systemic nature. As previously noted, in the study of organizational dynamics this approach provides an alternative lens to one that is purely rational and structural. By aligning our interventions with this approach, those who are in charge of organizations will obtain a greater awareness and understanding of their own behavior—why they do what they do—as well as the behavior of others; understanding is the most important tool in harnessing the potential of the people in the workplace. In addition, with the developmental perspective, we encourage our clients to gain greater insight into how past behavior, that may have been useful at an earlier stage of life, may no longer apply to their present situation. By helping our clients to become "clinicians" themselves, we hope to create more reflective practitioners.

> *By helping our clients to become "clinicians" themselves, we hope to create more reflective practitioners.*

By taking this psychodynamic-systemic clinical approach, we help our clients to acquire a holistic picture of what's going on in their particular situation. This enables them to become more aware and insightful of interpersonal and group behavior. By internalizing this clinical lens, over time our clients can become their own "organizational detectives," learning to uncover the nonrational patterns—the intrapsychic and interpersonal undercurrents—that influence the behavior of the individuals, dyads, and groups who they work with.

In fact, the use of this clinical approach can be seen as a "consciousness-raising" experience that cultivates our clients' self-understanding, deepens their understanding of others, and helps them to relate to society. With attention to behavioral patterns that may have their origin in earlier life experiences, our clients may arrive at the thematic unity to create meaning at multiple levels and determine the fundamental question of why they do what they do. When the link between past and present behavior establishes greater meaning, clients are more likely to reach the "tipping points" required for necessary change. As we have suggested, this unique clinical intervention can have team and organizational benefits beyond that of individual change. By drawing the unconscious origin of dysfunctional behavior patterns at the team and organizational level into consciousness, clients can address them directly and create healthier organizations with a more effective, self-fulfilled workforce.

> *When the link between past and present behavior establishes greater meaning, clients are more likely to reach the "tipping points" required for necessary change.*

3

Human Dilemmas in Leadership

Our destiny is frequently met in the very paths we take to avoid it.
—Jean de La Fontaine

Destiny is not a matter of chance; it is a matter of choice. It is not a thing to be waited for; it is a thing to be achieved.
—William Jennings Bryan

"Would you tell me, please, which way I ought to go from here?"
"That depends a good deal on where you want to get to," said the Cat.
"I don't much care where," said Alice.
"Then it doesn't matter which way you go," said the Cat.
—Lewis Carroll

Power Dynamics

The lion had been completely convinced of his dominance in the animal kingdom, but one day he wanted to check that all the other animals *knew* him to be the undisputed king of the jungle. He was so confident in his position that he decided not to talk to the smaller creatures and instead went straight to the buffalo. "Who is the king of the jungle?" asked the lion. The buffalo replied, "Of course, no one else but *you*, sir", at which the lion gave a great roar of approval. He continued on his way until he encountered the leopard, "Who is the king of the jungle?" he asked again. The leopard quickly responded, "All of us know that *you* are the king." The lion gave another roar of pleasure.

Next on his list was the elephant who he found at the edge of a river, and to who he asked the same question, "Who is the king of the jungle?" The elephant trumpeted, lifted his trunk, and grabbed the lion, throwing him into the air and smashing him into a tree. He fished him out of the tree and pounded him into the ground, lifted him up once more, and dumped him into the river. The elephant jumped once more on the drenched lion before dragging him through the mud, until he finally left him hanging from some bushes. The lion, dirty, beaten, bruised, and battered, struggled to get to his feet. He looked the elephant sadly in the eyes and said, "Look, just because you don't know the answer, that's no reason for you to be so mean-spirited about it."

The Narcissistic Temptation

There is a Chinese proverb which says: "Great men never feel great; small men never feel small." All too often, the gods destroy those who they had once called promising. Like the lion in the vignette to this chapter, many senior executives fail as a result of their narcissistic tendencies. Over-inflated by their position in life, they suffer from "hubris"—an ancient Greek word meaning excessive pride or unrestrained self-confidence. Or, simply put, they have become full of themselves.

> *All too often, the gods destroy those who they had once called promising.*

Hubris is rife in the context of leadership, as we have seen played out countless times; it is easy to forget that when organizations go down the drain, the rot frequently starts at the top. Or, to use the words of one wit, the bottleneck is all too often in the neck. Like the lion, successful individuals are prone to hubris; they grow self-centered and estranged from the concept of humility. In this way, they end up caught in the web of narcissistic behavior, in which everything they do is centered around themselves. The hubristic individual typically loses the ability to consider more creative ways of doing things and they become seemingly unable to metabolize their narcissistic disposition into empathy, compassion, humor, wisdom, and creativity. By starting to believe their own press, they are actually creating their own reality.

> *Hubris is rife in the context of leadership ... and having created their own reality, hubristic individuals are rarely receptive to change.*

Narcissism may cause individuals to become fixated on issues of power, status, prestige, and superiority. They may be unwilling to tolerate disagreement and criticism. They aren't prepared to consult others for their opinions—narcissistic leaders don't give other people a voice. But if senior executives are unwilling to listen to the people who work for them, or reassess their decisions and actions, how can they expect to get the best out of people?

> *Narcissism and leadership often go hand in hand; the more power individuals are given, the more inclined they are to become narcissistic.*

Due to the egotistical behavior of leaders of this nature, it is common that the people around them will only tell them what they like to hear. They start to live in an echo chamber because people will have learnt that critical observations are ignored, and their leader has become too self-involved to listen. As a result, from within this narcissistic bubble, their grasp of reality will be impaired or distorted. And a factor that exasperates or consolidates a narcissistic leader's skewed realities is that many of their associates struggle with the nature of the evolving group dynamics and simply agree with what they say, regardless of its accuracy or realism.

Having created their own reality, hubristic individuals are rarely receptive to change. Like the lion, they are inclined to hold on to a specific set of ideals, or logic, regardless of how illogical they may turn out to be. They lack the emotional intelligence to be objective, and don't want, or recognize, the need for change.

What we wish to make clear is that narcissism and leadership often go hand in hand; the more power individuals are given, the more inclined they are to become narcissistic. There are countless examples in which this combination of disposition and position can, and has become, toxic, contributing to inappropriate, destructive behavior. Hence, it is a leader's ultimate responsibility to be vigilant to the warning signs of narcissistic thinking; in this, humility is their greatest countervailing power.

> *It is a leader's ultimate responsibility to be vigilant to the warning signs of narcissistic thinking; in this, humility is their greatest countervailing power.*

With this in mind, while coaching and consulting, we always pay considerable attention to the existing power dynamics when employing organizational interventions. The role the powerholders—prime candidates for narcissistic tendencies—play will always be forefront in our minds. That is not to say we disregard the role played by other organizational participants, only that we are realistic about which roles in organizations are likely to be the greatest challenge and require the most significant change. We need to understand what is going on in the minds of the people in charge of the organizations that we deal with.

Change Resistances

It is not always easy to establish why many executives cling so tenaciously to their views, or why they provide the most conscious and unconscious obstacles in working toward change. The wise proverb that warns "All things change, and we change with them" seemingly doesn't apply in their case, and their dependence on dysfunctional behavior patterns can be particularly devastating. Given the power senior executives wield, their behavior can have a dramatic downward ripple effect within an organization, cultivating a toxic corporate culture, impaired or inept decision-making processes, and motivational problems. Subsequently, such organizations may well have a high turnover of employees, deterred or frustrated by their stress-carrying leader.

> *Many senior executives either forget, or are not adequately cognizant of the fact, that they are always on stage in their organization.*

What senior executives, especially CEOs, may not realize is that their seemingly innocuous actions can have dramatic consequences. Many either forget, or are not adequately cognizant of the fact, that they are always on stage in their organization. Any action they take will be carefully observed, analyzed, and discussed among their employees, and often further afield.

This brings to mind an observation made by a senior executive during one of our change interventions. He noted: "Every day I come into the office knowing I can make the lives of my thousands of employees quite miserable. Unfortunately, it doesn't take very much to do so. Realizing this, however, makes for an awesome responsibility. I need to keep reminding myself daily of the symbolic role that I also play."

In this age of discontinuity, the power that senior executives possess can affect the lives of large numbers of people, and therefore it is more important than ever to help them make the right decisions. Naturally, this raises the question as to what we, in a consultancy or coaching role, can do to help these senior executives manage their roles in the most exemplary fashion. What can we do to make them more effective? How can we help them to create healthy, sustainable organizations? If changes in their behavior patterns are required, how should we go about doing it?

> *In this age of discontinuity, the power that senior executives possess can affect the lives of large numbers of people, and therefore it is more important than ever to help them make the right decisions.*

We recognize that a leader's role is far from easy. For many, being in charge of an organization is a daunting task and many appear overwhelmed by the responsibility that comes with their position. Often, they aren't even clear what role they should play and need all the help they can get to define this and be effective in it.

When moving into a leadership position, many individuals realize that it isn't easy to get the best out of their people. To motivate their people toward progress and development can be challenging and many leaders don't know how to stimulate their employees' imagination and "stretch" themselves collectively. They may also be unable to communicate the dreams they have for the future of the organization.

We have seen how senior executives can cling stubbornly to dysfunctional behavior patterns, ignore constructive suggestions, and reject change, often with dismal consequences. What we should realize, however, is that many live with the perverse hope that while continuing to do the same thing over and over again, the outcome might be somewhat different. Obviously, they are not familiar with the old Sioux Indian saying: "when you discover that you are riding a dead horse, the best strategy is to dismount." On the contrary, given their behavior, some senior executives seem to hang on to the unrealistic fantasy that they would be able to resuscitate the horse.

> *There is a tendency amongst people who claim to believe in the importance of change to make only half-hearted efforts towards it: deep down they don't really want to change themselves, but would rather others change to suit them.*

What we have observed is a tendency among people who claim to believe in the importance of change to make only half-hearted efforts towards it. Deep down, they don't really want to change themselves, but would rather others change to suit them. In fact, for many people in an organization, change implies a loss of the security that comes with a specific job. They fear the unknown, become anxious, and cling to old patterns of behavior. Some executives are concerned that they will lose their sense of freedom; others fear that change will result in a loss of responsibility, authority, rights, privileges, or status; others still may interpret change as an indictment of their past performance and react defensively. Unexplained change may also threaten existing alliances, implying the loss of important friends and contacts. As with any of these situations, the fear of leaving familiar people and surroundings can arouse profound insecurities and subsequent resistance. For those executives who deal with budgets, there is also the question of sunk costs: they may be reluctant to accept a change that entails scrapping certain costly investments; a feared decrease in income will almost always be met with resistance.

The behavioral patterns we refer to here are reminiscent of a Calvin & Hobbes' cartoon (Calvin being a young boy and Hobbes his toy tiger), in which Calvin says, "I thrive on change," and Hobbes, surprised by this statement, says: "You?! You threw a fit this morning because your mom put less jelly on your toast than yesterday!"[1] To which Calvin responds, "I thrive on making other people change."

> Un*learning* can be one of the greatest challenges.

In some of these situations, people may not always resist change, but they may well be baffled by it. Perhaps these individuals have the will but not the skill to change. Their concerns—often stemming from a fear of failure—revolve around the question of whether they are competent enough to cope with more or different expectations arising from change. The British

---

[1] Bill Watterson (1993, April 16). *Calvin & Hobbes*. Kansas City, MO: Universal Press Syndicate.

economist John Maynard Keynes put this more succinctly when he said, "The difficulty lies, not in the new ideas, but in escaping from the old ones, which ramify, for those brought up as most of us have been, into every corner of our minds."[2] In reality, *un*learning can be one of the greatest challenges. The recurrent point, exemplified by the story of the lion, is that narcissistic tendencies—the hubristic sense of knowing better—are prevalent in the field of leadership, and can severely hamper any change-making initiative.

The EQ Factor

Having worked with thousands of senior executives, we have concluded that another major reason why we encounter so much resistance to change is a lack of emotional intelligence (EQ). By this we mean the ability to understand and manage our emotions as well as recognize emotions in others and handle relationships with sensitivity. A lack of emotional intelligence suggests an underlying lack of self-understanding. In order to be effective as a leader, possessing emotional intelligence is a sine qua non.

> *A lack of emotional intelligence suggests an underlying lack of self-understanding.*

Executives, or in fact anyone in a leadership position, who lack emotional intelligence will be severely constrained in their effectiveness. This can manifest in any number of counterproductive ways. As we have outlined, narcissistic behavior commonly hampers their objectivity and their ability to make informed decisions. They may become more interested in constructing their media presence, losing interest in the nitty-gritty aspect of management, and becoming "leaders in orbit." This may contribute to problems in prioritizing and deciding what is important. They may become conflict-avoidant entirely, or suffer decision paralysis, in which they cannot make necessary tough decisions; in all cases, letting things slip can have disastrous consequences.

On the flip side, they may also become micro-managers, compelled to control every aspect of their organization without delegating or making others accountable. Furthermore, some of the clients we work with simply don't know how to inspire, energize, and get the best out of their people in working

---

[2] John Maynard Keynes (1936). "Preface". In *The General Theory of Employment, Interest and Money*. Cambridge and London: Cambridge University Press, for the Royal Economic Society.

toward a common goal. In all these scenarios, they are resorting to behavioral patterns that may once have proved effective but are no longer relevant to their present situation. Without the emotional intelligence key to recognizing these patterns, they are at risk of becoming self-destructive.

Finding the Leader Within

When people feel stuck, it is our responsibility as executive coaches and consultants to help them out of their self-imposed prison. By developing their EQ we can encourage a better understanding of both themselves and others. To become more open to experience requires us to teach them how to go beyond purely logical, analytical thinking and learn how to "play" again.

> *What clients need to realize is that a realistic change process starts with a willingness to change themselves.*

What clients need to realize is that a realistic change process starts with a willingness to change themselves. Leadership starts within; it is, above all, "an *inside* job." People interested in leadership positions need to acknowledge the importance of exploring their personal journey in order to understand more about themselves. Becoming a more effective leader requires a lot of introspection. Those who are prepared to undertake this inner journey may be surprised by what they learn. They may establish their own strengths and weaknesses and what they really want out of life. In other words, those seeking to reinvent themselves need to develop a high degree of self-awareness and self-knowledge, and that only occurs when they start looking at what's happening inside themselves.

> *Those seeking to reinvent themselves need to develop a high degree of self-awareness and self-knowledge, and that only occurs when they start looking at what's happening inside themselves.*

By self-awareness we mean perceiving, knowing, feeling, or being conscious of events, objects, thoughts, or sensory patterns. If they're able to do this in interpersonal and group encounters, they will understand better their own behaviors, emotions, beliefs, and values. Effectively, self-awareness refers to a real-time understanding of one's emotional and mental states. In comparison, self-knowledge refers to knowledge acquired through experience. It means being cognizant not only of one's strengths and weaknesses, but the intricate motivations, desires, and fears that drive them. The process necessitates delving deep into a person's unconscious and peeling back the layers to reveal the core of their identity.

Socrates pointed out the importance of self-knowledge as early as 399 BC when he noted, "The unexamined life is not worth living."[3] Thus, a willingness to engage in continuous self-exploration creates an openness to change. Consequently, it will be a sine qua non for people in responsible executive positions. In fact, open mindedness, flexibility, curiosity, and playfulness are some of the attributes that make for healthy living and creativity in executive life.

> *Self-awareness refers to a real-time understanding of one's emotional and mental states. In comparison, self-knowledge refers to knowledge acquired through experience.*

The Reinvention Process

Our challenge as coaches and consultants is to help executives find ways to reinvent themselves. We need to help them to pay attention to the psychological forces that affect them most and encourage them to be more open to new experiences. As successful leadership tends to be a team sport, this means leaders must become highly attuned to the needs of others. Not only do executives require the ability to function effectively in teams, but they also must know *how* those teams are built in the first place.

As coaches and consultants, we can help them to work on their EQ and initiate a ripple effect to manage other patterns of behavior. Not only will this improve their vision of where they want their organization to go, but it will also affect the actions that they will take. Vision without proper execution is something of a hallucination. As the writer Ernest Hemingway once said, "Never confuse movement with action."[4]

---

[3] Plato (2000/c.399–387 BC). "The Apology." In *The Trial and Death of Socrates: Euthyphro, Apology, Crito, Death Scene from Phaedo*. Trans. G.M.A. Grube. Indianapolis, IN: Hackett Publishing.
[4] A.E. Hotchner (2005). *Papa Hemingway: A Personal Memoir*. Cambridge, MA: Da Capo Press.

> *Vision without proper execution is something of a hallucination.*

We thus suggest, albeit in a glib way, that effective executives master the seven Cs of managerial behavior: they must be **self-Confident** (a factor on which all the other ones depend). There must also be a deep **Commitment** to whatever they're doing. They must know how to handle **Complexity**, possess **Creativity**, meaning being able to think out of the box, and have the **Courage** to make difficult decisions. Furthermore, they express a great **Concern** about their people, and to do so as great **Communicators**.

The inevitable question, therefore, is first how to help senior executives acquire the necessary skills to adapt this "7 C model" to their own situation, and, secondly, how can we help them to modify dysfunctional behavior patterns? Here, we emphasize again how applying the clinical paradigm can be of value, and why, as coaches and consultants, we need to try to be wise counselors to our clients, helping them acquire a greater understanding of their own behavior as well as that of others. In this respect, we subscribe to the statement of the Greek philosopher, Xenophanes, who once said, "It takes a wise man to discover a wise man."[5]

---

[5] Diogenes Laërtius (1853/third century AD). "Xenophanes." In *The Lives and Opinions of Eminent Philosophers*. Trans. C.D. Yonge. London: Henry G. Bohn.

4

Socio-dynamics

If any man is able to convince me and show me that I do not think or act right, I will gladly change; for I seek the truth by which no man was ever injured. But he is injured who abides in his error and ignorance.
—Marcus Aurelius

Ye live not for yourselves; ye cannot live for yourselves; a thousand fibres connect you with your fellow-men, and along those fibres, as along sympathetic threads, run your actions as causes, and return to you as effects.
—Henry Melville

If I have seen further, it is by standing on the shoulders of giants.
—Isaac Newton

The Four Bulls and the Lion

There is a well-known fable by the legendary Greek storyteller, Aesop,[1] about four bulls and a lion. In this tale, a lion prowled about a field in which four bulls dwelt. He had tried to attack them many times, but whenever he approached, they turned their tails to one another, so that, whichever way he neared them, he was met by at least one of the bulls' horns. At last,

---

[1] Aesop (620–564 BC). *The Bulls and the Lion.* Perry Index, fable 372.

perceiving that he had no chance as long as they stuck together, the lion realized that he needed to create conflict among the bulls. He had to have them act dysfunctionally as a group. At long last, perceiving no attempt was to be made upon the bulls as long as this combination held, the lion managed, through subtle whispers and hints, to turn the four bulls against each other. They began to quarrel, which caused them to retreat to the pasture alone, each one of them grazing in a separate corner of the field. It was at this point that the lion attacked them one by one and soon brought an end to all four.

The Psychodynamics of Groups

To make executives effective and create great places to work, the people who lead organizations need to have a deep understanding of what happens when groups of people come together. Thus, deciphering the interactions and interpersonal relationships between members of a group and the ways in which groups form, function, and dissolve themselves must to take center stage. Hence, an understanding of group dynamics can help clients decipher the intricacies of organizational life.

The British psychoanalyst and psychiatrist Wilfred Bion identified three basic assumptions that will pass through people's minds in a group setting—**dependency**, **fight–flight**, and **pairing**.[2] These are all activities that may result in pathological regressive processes, which deflect people from the principal tasks that have to be performed.

> *Dependency, fight–flight, and pairing are all activities that may result in pathological regressive processes, which deflect people from the principal tasks that have to be performed.*

When we deconstruct these basic assumptions that occur in a group setting, it becomes apparent that people often assume—at an unconscious level—that those who lead organizations should offer protection and guidance similar to what should have been offered by their parents in their developmental years. Here, life history seems to repeat itself. For example, like children, groups subjected to the ***dependency assumption*** are united by feelings of helplessness, inadequacy, neediness, and fear of the outside world.

---

[2] Wilfred R. Bion (1961). *Experiences in Groups and Other Papers*. London: Routledge.

To overcome these feelings, they would like to perceive their leaders as effectively omnipotent; to view them as their possible protectors, expected to give them guidance. But this willingness to be guided implies also a willingness to let go of their independence. It could cause them to be reluctant when it comes to taking any initiative and may even impact their critical judgment. On the plus side, however, this preparedness to give up their autonomy can make for a sense of goal-directedness and cohesiveness.

> *People often assume—at an unconscious level—that those who lead organizations should offer protection and guidance similar to what should have been offered by their parents in their developmental years.*

Another common unconscious assumption that occurs in groups is that the organizational world is viewed as inherently dangerous. In light of this feeling, those working in organizations may resort to fight or flight as a defense mechanism. When groups operate under this **fight–flight assumption** there will be a tendency to split the world into camps of friend or foe. Because they are now subscribing to a rigid, bipolar view of the world, those working in organizations will tend to possess a strong desire for protection from and conquest of "the enemy." Some leaders actually encourage the fight–flight assumption, inflaming their followers against real and/or imagined enemies, and using the in-group/out-group division to motivate people and to channel anxiety outward. There is however one potentially positive outcome of this outlook on the world in that it can reinforce group identity and create meaning for those who may otherwise feel lost. The resulting sense of unity is highly reassuring, but it does make the group increasingly dependent on their leader.

Bion's third assumption is that pairing up with a person or subgroup perceived as powerful will help a person cope with anxiety, alienation, and loneliness. People experiencing the **pairing assumption** fantasize that strength will take place in pairs. Unfortunately, pairing also implies splitting, which may result in intragroup and intergroup conflict and the building of smaller systems within the group. It also manifests itself in ganging up against the leader, who is perceived as an aggressor or authority figure.

> *A group of people will unconsciously collude to protect themselves against the anxiety and tension that exists in their workplace, despite the fact that this often inhibits what the organization is trying to accomplish.*

Social Defense Mechanisms

Given the dangerous world we live in, organizational life is filled with angst and unpredictability. When these organizational anxieties aren't properly managed, various defensive reactions will come to the fore. The people working in these organizations may resort to these three basic assumptions. In addition, they may also act out and engage in regressive "social defenses" to transform and neutralize the prevailing depressive and paranoid feelings of anxiety they are experiencing. As opposed to individual defense mechanisms such as splitting and projection, social defenses can be looked at as aspects of organizations that exist independently of its members. Usually, they are represented as structures and policies that serve to reinforce the organizational participants' defenses against the primitive anxieties encountered in the workplace. In other words, a group of people will unconsciously collude to protect themselves against the anxiety and tension that exists in their workplace, despite the fact that this often inhibits what the organization is trying to accomplish.

Typically, executives rely on existing structures and processes to "contain" their anxiety. But when these ways of dealing with organizational anxieties become the dominant mode of operation (rather than an occasional stopgap measure), they become dysfunctional for the organization as a whole by creating bureaucratic obstacles. Task forces, administrative procedures, and other structures and processes are used to keep people emotionally uninvolved and to help them feel safe and in control. Furthermore, these bureaucratic routines and pseudo-rational activities can also obscure personal and organizational realities, allowing people to detach themselves by replacing creativity, empathy, awareness, and openness to change with control and impersonality.

> *A 'folie à deux' collusion between leader and follower manifests itself as a form of a shared madness that can turn into mass organizational insanity.*

Folie à deux

When we adopt a more macro perspective to the prevailing group dynamics in organizations, one troubling dynamic that can be observed in specific leader–follower relationships is what has been described as a "*folie à deux*" collusion. This manifests itself as a form of a shared madness that can turn into mass organizational insanity. In such collusions, there is usually a dominant person whose irrational behavior has become adopted by other members of the organization. In other words, leaders whose capacity for reality testing has become impaired may transfer their delusionary ideas to their followers, who in order to minimize conflict and disagreement will sacrifice truth and honest criticism to maintain a connection with the leader, even though he or she has lost touch with reality. In extreme cases, a *folie à deux* can lead to the self-destruction of the leader, professionally speaking, and to the collective demise of his or her followers.

> *Leaders whose capacity for reality testing has become impaired may transfer their delusionary ideas to their followers, …who will sacrifice truth and honest criticism to maintain a connection with the leader, even though he or she has lost touch with reality.*

At the same time, in our consultancy and coaching activities we also subscribe to the ideas of Miguel de Cervantes, the author of the Spanish epic novel *Don Quixote*, who once wrote that "our greatest foes, and whom we must chiefly combat, are within."[3] He argued that change cannot occur without a certain dose of madness. Essentially, without a little madness, it is hard to think out of the box. We also think that a small dose of madness in organizational life could contribute to a break-through. What we are also suggesting is that we should never lose this spark of madness within.

> *Without a little madness, it is hard to think out of the box.*

Having said that, it is worth pointing out that the madness of Don Quixote, the hero of de Cervantes' epic, was built on his inability to discern fact from fiction. In his case, he had read so many tales of chivalry that he took them to be real, and then cast himself as a knight errant and his present world as the scene of an epic. In our coaching sessions, where we listen intently to our clients, we also find ourselves at times thrown into a world in which the line between narrative and historical truth appears to be blurred—not unlike what Don Quixote experienced. This is especially true

---

[3] Miguel de Cervantes (1865/1605). *The History of the Ingenious Gentleman Don Quixote of la Mancha*. Translated from the Spanish by Motteux. With copious notes, and essay on the life and writings of Cervantes, by John G. Lockhart. Boston, MA: Little, Brown and Company, Vol 3, p. 78.

in the present digital world where discerning fact from fiction has become increasingly difficult. That is why we continue to emphasize the importance of the clinical approach as a means of helping us stay close to reality.

5

The Coaching Conundrum

A soldier who is arrogant cannot conquer.
—Lao Tzu

Tell the antecedents, knows the present, and foretell the future.
—Hippocrates

Every man is liable to err; it is the part only of a fool to persevere in error.
—Marcus Tullius Cicero

The Two Monks and the King

There is a Zen story about two monks who visited a king. When the king asked the monks if they would be able to teach him the way of Zen, the first monk said to the king that, given his wisdom, he would have an innate ability to become an expert in Zen. Listening to this, the second monk reprimanded the first, saying: "What idiocy, why do you flatter this person. He may be a king, but he knows nothing about Zen."

Hearing what both monks had said, the king built a temple. It was not for the first monk, but rather the second, realizing that he would be the one best able to teach him the way of Zen.

What Is Executive Coaching All About?

As we can see from the vignette, whereas one of the monks was prepared to engage in a *folie à deux*, the other kept a cool head. He wasn't intimidated by power and riches, nor was he willing to regress into a shared form of madness. Being able to maintain this kind of internal equilibrium is not something that comes easily and, for many in the modern world of business, it is often developed and enhanced through the coaching process. While there are those who may feel turning to a coach is a sign of weakness, it is important to remember that nobody is an island. We are social creatures and, as such, we benefit from being in dialogue with each other. And it is here where executive coaching enters the scene.

But what is executive coaching all about? Generally speaking, coaching can be considered a specific type of intervention that can be carried out strategically with individuals and/or teams or the total organization. Its aim is to direct a person or group of people toward a specific, mutually determined goal, accelerating their progress by providing focus and awareness. It is about helping the people who are being coached to actualize their strengths and minimize their weaknesses. In other words, to help them attain their full potential. The challenge is to have these people reach a point whereby they not only know themselves better, but also feel comfortable with who they are and what they do. Hence, as coaches, we want them to be more effective in dealing with others. And executive coaching has proven to be a great way to build executives' confidence and competence.

> *Executive coaching is about helping those who are being coached to actualize their strengths and minimize their weaknesses.*

What needs to be added is that historically coaches were assigned to people considered to be ineffective in their job. But that is no longer the case. In our current environment, executive coaching has gone beyond being merely a remedial activity. It is not just about identifying and dealing with dysfunctionality. Rather, it has become much more about assessing where the executives in their particular organizations are now and where they want to be, including gaps in that progression that may need to be addressed.

The real challenge for present-day executive coaches is to have more of a systemic outlook, taking the context into consideration. To be effective, they need to develop a helicopter view, not merely an atomistic or individually based orientation. In addition, to continue this more macro-orientation, they should provide structures for goal setting and standards of accountability. To be true agents of individual, cultural, and organizational change, executive coaches need to have a big-picture focus.

> *To be effective, executive coaches need to develop a helicopter view, not merely an atomistic or individually based orientation.*

To enable these transformations, present-day executive coaches have to make sure that emerging resistances are dealt with. In their role as change agents, they should be prepared to work with their clients to create realistic action plans. In addition, they need to focus on follow-up to be sure that the planned progress is indeed occurring, and, if not, to figure out why that's not the case. In other words, in our day-and-age, coaching focuses on helping good people and their organizations become even better at becoming more proficient at managing their careers and their life.

Splitters and Bundlers

Executive coaching has been described in many different ways. In that respect, we can talk about "splitters" and "bundlers." For example, some are quite adamant about separating or "splitting" performance, skills, career, and life coaching. Others draw very specific lines between coaching and consulting, even though these differences quite easily can become blurred. Often, coaching may also morph into consulting and vice versa. With our clinical approach, however, we think these various forms of coaching and consulting easily blend into each other and thus bundling them makes the most sense. That said, we do differentiate between individual and group coaching interventions.

The growth of one-to-one coaching has been much faster than group coaching, mostly because the latter is more difficult, not as clearly scoped, and is a less well understood concept in organizational life. The reason is self-evident. Because of the web of interpersonal relationships, group coaching is not for the faint of heart. Consequently, given its complexity, it doesn't come as a great surprise that executive coaching is mostly carried out on an individual basis. Clearly, the group coach has to deal with many psychodynamic and systemic forces that do not occur when coaching on an individual basis. In fact, effective group coaches need to be masters in the kind of paradoxes that are so ubiquitous in organizational life.

> *Effective group coaches need to be masters in the kind of paradoxes that are so ubiquitous in organizational life.*

The differences between individual coaching and group coaching are notable. While in individual coaching questions focus on performance, skill, career development, individual motivation, identity, and authenticity, group coaching ups the ante by adding such topics as shared team or organizational purpose, better collaboration, the need for silo busting, the issue of knowledge management, the creation of more open forms of communication, enhancing creativity, and the need for external networking. Consequently, to coach groups of people simultaneously, the focus needs to be on interpersonal skills and group dynamics instead of merely on individual development (as we tend to do with individually focused coaching).

> *The role of the executive coach is to identify the "undiscussables" and, by acknowledging them and bringing them out into the open, make them discussable.*

In particular, group coaches face the challenge of simultaneously having to make sense of the needs of the individual in the group and the dynamics of the group-as-a-whole, including how people in a collaborative setting communicate with one another. In reference to the morality tale of the lion and the four bulls, they should be astute enough to recognize emerging "groupthink" processes such as illusions of invulnerability, pressures to conform, illusions of unanimity, self-censorship, and the use of mind-guards. Recognizing conflictual interpersonal situations, as well as what and where these conflicts arise, is also critical. Some of these issues may originate within the team as a whole or just with specific individuals. For example, it could be that there is person ill-suited to the job assigned and so lacks the competencies to perform the job well. However, the problem can just as easily be a systemic one, whereby the organizational architecture does not foster a trusting, well-balanced team. As more individuals begin to suspect that things aren't working as they should, they may refrain from talking about it. In fact, there may arise certain "undiscussables"—topics that seem to be taboo and may hinder the effective operation of the organization. Here, the role of the executive coach is to identify these "undiscussables" and, by acknowledging them and bringing them out into the open, make them discussable.

If group coaching is done well, it will help people understand how to work better with others and will thus become an effective method for showing the members of an organization how to reduce conflict and improve their working relationships. Consequently, the organizational participants can then focus on the organization's real work and achieve its objectives.

Internal Versus External

Another important distinction in the coaching used by organizations is that between internal or external leadership coaches. Internal coaches tend to be employees of the organization, whereas external coaches are contracted to work with the organization. Although internal coaches will be more familiar with the ins-and-outs of the organization, leaders working with them may have concerns about confidentiality. Clearly, for leadership coaching to be most effective, there must be absolute trust between the parties involved. This means that the individuals who are being coached must feel certain that their exchanges with the coach will remain confidential and will not affect their employment or status within the organization.

> *For leadership coaching to be most effective, there must be absolute trust between the parties involved.*

The Objectives of Individual Coaching

In our approach to coaching we don't necessarily make a clear distinction between skills and performance coaching, career coaching, transition coaching, "legacy" coaching, life coaching, "on-boarding" coaching, or other supposedly specialized fields of individual coaching. In addition, there is also the question of coaching morphing into more directive consulting. In fact, we find many of these distinctions quite artificial. We tend to have a much more holistic approach to the client. But whatever we do, we try to tailor our coaching to the specific needs of our clients. And in working with our clients, they have listed many of the benefits we provide, as summarized in the box below:

> **The Benefits of Individual Coaching as Indicated by Clients**
>
> *Individual coaching can help a recipient to:*
>
> - Learn how to work smarter, not harder, knowing where the greatest contribution can be made
> - Find ways of communicating with greater clarity
> - Learn how to become more adaptable and successful in dealing with change
> - Increase the ability to respond more skillfully to organizational challenges and opportunities
> - Become more effective in conflict resolution
> - Recognize blind spots and defensive patterns
> - Turn personal awareness into insight and that insight into action
> - Understand better the perceptions of other organizational participants
> - Be more assertive and self-confident
> - Improve existing superior–subordinate relationships
> - Learn to manage upward better
> - Become more effective in giving and receiving feedback
> - Become a better (more active) listener
> - Lower levels of stress and increase the sense of enjoying the work
> - Be able to coach the people within the organization, when appropriate
> - Become better at finding creative solutions to knotty problems
> - Become more effective in managing paradoxical situations
> - Build stronger, more trusting relationships
> - Show a more authentic leadership style
> - Be successful in a new role
> - Work on the development of emotional intelligence
> - Establish stronger relationships with clients
> - Be more deliberate in developing a career development plan, making an in-depth assessment of what is currently working and not working
> - Identify really meaningful life goals
> - Take a greater sense of ownership and responsibility for behaviors and actions
> - Be successful in the creation of a legacy
> - Acquire a better work–life balance

We have always imagined that by providing individual coaching, we are providing a place where the client's private self can be heard, honored, and challenged. But also, in our role as coaches we try to offer each client the opportunity to create the space for their vision, help them to set clearly defined goals that support that vision, and have them evaluate the results.

> *People are less likely to resist change if their anxieties are acknowledged and they are offered developmental opportunities to assuage their self-doubt.*

Moving with the Resistances

Although coaching interventions can help to lessen people's anxiety about change and increase their feelings of authenticity and self-efficacy, the fact is that when individuals and groups perceive change as a threat, they will resist it, however positive it may appear. Individuals may also doubt their ability to make the changes needed, or believe that the status quo is good enough. Thus, when people in an organization are driven by fear or held back by incomprehension, a toxic culture is created that may eventually destroy the company. However, it's important to note that people are less likely to resist change if their anxieties are acknowledged and they are offered developmental opportunities to assuage their self-doubt.

> *Successful change management is not only about doing new things but is also about new ways of looking at things.*

In the coaching process we help our clients realize that successful change management is not only about doing new things but is also about new ways of looking at things. We point out that the process of inquiry never stops. It is because of this continual need for learning that executive coaching can become such a powerful force. As the Russian novelist Leo Tolstoy once said, "Everybody thinks of changing humanity, and nobody thinks of changing himself."[1] As change agents, we support people in changing their perception of reality, encouraging them to realize that change within the world and within themselves is inevitable.

---

[1] Leo Tolstoy (1900). "Three Methods of Reform." In *Letters to Friends on the Personal Christian Life*. Christchurch, Hants: The Free Age Press.

6

Teams and Company

By perseverance the snail reached the ark.
—Proverb

This world is the mountain, and our action the shout: the echo of the shouts comes back to us.
—Rúmí

It is better to have a Lyon at the Head of an Army of Sheep; than a Sheep at the Head of an Army of Lyons.
—Anon

The King's Palace

There is a Zen story about a mighty king who built his palace without windows for fear that his enemies would reach him. There was only one door, guarded by a large number of soldiers.

Then one day, surrounded by his guards, the king went out for a walk and encountered a Zen master by the roadside who laughed at him.

"What is there to laugh about?" asked the king angrily.

"The door is still open to your enemies," said the Zen master. "You need to brick it up."

"But," the king said, "my palace would then turn into a tomb."

"But it is a tomb already," replied the Zen master. "By eliminating doors and windows, you are preventing people to enter. You are eliminating life.

Widen the doors! Widen them until the walls are no more. Be brave enough to deal with groups of people. That is life!"

How Effective Are Teams?

As we try to point out using this Zen story as an example, although individual coaching has an important role in an executive coach's intervention repertoire, and individual interventions are clearly valuable, it doesn't create the same intensity, focus, and push toward change that can be achieved through group forms of coaching. In that respect, working with groups of people has many advantages, particularly if it concerns executive teams. In these situations, the coaching client becomes the whole team as a system rather than each of the executives in turn. This kind of intervention focuses on helping every one of the team members to change their interaction patterns, yet still taking into consideration the individual personalities that are part of the team. When successful, this form of group coaching ensures that the members of a team will have a more constructive way of dealing with one other. By contrast, in one-on-one coaching, follow-up is conducted by executive coaches who are often available irregularly, leaving individual organizational leaders to get things done very much on their own. Hence, coaching in a group setting tends to speed up change processes and in these kinds of interventions we try very hard to capture the collective wisdom of the group.

At the same time, however, we are very aware that teams are complex entities and we recognize that team dynamics can be very hard to handle. But we also know that the relationships between the team members will often be the deciding factor between an organization's success and failure. Thus, we emphasize that there is much strength in unity. Each time we embark on this kind of venture we keep in mind the African proverb "If you want to go fast, go alone. If you want to go far, go together." If the team members work properly together, the whole is going to be greater than the sum of its parts. We are also cognizant of the fact that, given the importance of working in teams in contemporary network-oriented organizations, the use of teamwork is only going to increase, virtually or otherwise. Teams will therefore take on an increasingly important role, and many of these teams will be seeking the support of experienced group coaches to improve their effectiveness.

> *The relationships between the team members will often be the deciding factor between an organization's success and failure.*

Of course, in the case of leadership teams, the people working in the team have to make a choice. Are they willing to harness the collective wisdom of the team? Do they all want to pull together, doing whatever they can to achieve a combined success? Or will the members of the team just go through the motions, merely pretending to be a team? Overt and covert conflict may very well be the reason for pseudo-team behavior. In fact, when a team is dysfunctional, we can observe how its members can find themselves in a situation where discussions become endless and end up going nowhere—the team just doesn't seem to gel and people are just going through the motions.

> *Given the importance of working in teams in contemporary network-oriented organizations, the use of teamwork is only going to increase, virtually or otherwise.*

The challenge for executive coaches, therefore, is to move the members of a team off "cruise control" and place them into more of a "manual operation." They need to acquire a sense of ownership. Hence, as change catalysts, our task is to help our clients develop the skills that make for better team interaction and collaboration—with an end goal to create the best companies to work for. But to do so, we need to help them to discover their shared values and objectives. To acquire such a collaborative mindset, however, implies that the team members will need to improve their communication and listening skills and, not surprisingly, it hence becomes necessary for the members of the team to develop their emotional intelligence.

If they become more emotionally intelligent—if they become adept in the soft skills—they will be more equipped in dealing with the unfinished business or baggage between the members of their team. Part of the emotional intelligence equation is to create an organizational culture in which its members trust each other and are willing to be vulnerable. In other words, they should be prepared to admit that they don't always know everything and that they may need the help of others to accomplish what needs to be done. Basically, they need to recognize that teamwork will be a vital way for organizations to be viable.

However, although we realize the importance of teamwork, we are also not naïve. Some team situations can be quite indomitable. Sometimes, we may need to resort to other kinds of intervention. Consequently, in every situation, we first have to assess how effective the teams we're dealing with really are. We must assess whether the situation in the company is so dire that a group intervention by itself won't achieve the desired results and more dramatic steps are necessary. For example, given the existing power dynamics, could a more substantial structural or strategic change be more appropriate?

Whatever we decide to do, however, we start with the premise that in most instances working as a team will be a good thing, knowing that if an effective team is in place, people can be highly productive and creative. In fact, when observing a high-performance team in action, we can see how people's self-confidence grows. We see how they enjoy working together. We notice how the members of the team are creating a sense of community and how they find meaning in whatever they are doing. Essentially, the members of the team are on task and things get done.

> *In a well-functioning team, its members are focused on what needs to be done. They subscribe to the organizational goals. They stand behind its values.*

In a well-functioning team, its members are focused on what needs to be done. They subscribe to the organizational goals. They stand behind its values. To enable a productive interface between the members of the team, there is in place a facilitating form of leadership that appreciates the contribution of all its members. In addition, in these instances, the role assignments will fit each member's capabilities. Furthermore, there exists mutual respect between the members of the team and a relationship pattern that makes for constructive conflict resolution. There are also clear measures of success and personal accountability as well as a power within the team to make decisions. Moreover, during the discussions, process and content are taken into consideration. Time is taken to reflect on the prevailing team dynamics. In these teams, a learning environment has also been created that furthers the organization's growth. Consequently, in the process, team members will arrive at greater self-understanding and better self-management skills, which, in turn, will lead to greater creativity, as well as more thoughtful decisions and inspired career choices.

> *Many teams can be highly "constipated" and conflicted bodies, which contributes to slow decision-making.*

Team Dysfunctionality

Of course, what has been said about the characteristics of well-functioning teams tends to be more the exception than the rule. Unfortunately, what we have learned from our experiences is that many teams can be highly "constipated" and conflicted bodies, which contributes to slow decision-making. Many teams underperform in spite of all the resources available to them. To add insult to injury, all too often the outcomes of the team's decision-making turn out to be sub-optimal.

> *One major cause of dysfunctional team outcomes is the inability of the team members to work well together due to conflicts between the different personalities.*

There are many causes for these dysfunctional team outcomes, the major one being the inability of the team members to work well together due to conflicts between the different personalities. There may be a lack of understanding or appreciation of each team member. There may be poor communication. In addition, there may be dysfunctional power dynamics at play. In particular, top executives can play a highly dysfunctional role by putting people on certain teams for purely political reasons—creating teams in name only.

Essentially, when competitive feelings dominate and people approach a team with a win–lose attitude, personal motives will rule and the interests of the organization will tend to become secondary: the team members will put their individual needs above the needs of the group. When this is the case, every choice and every decision will be affected greatly by the influence and future plans of each of its members. At the same time, a tension will exist between the cooperation needed to work as team and the implicit competition of the people in the team who are out for their own interests.

Often, in these dysfunctional teams, there are many "undiscussables" as well as covert and overt conflicts that the members are afraid to address. Consequently, such teams may be characterized by fuzzy goals and changing priorities. Their tasks may be poorly defined. People are not accountable and there may be uneven participation. Furthermore, given these dysfunctional team dynamics, team meetings become of a calcified nature. People will drift in and out, or won't come at all. And if they are present, they are often poorly prepared. Decisions are badly thought through or even not made.

> *Top executives can play a highly dysfunctional role by putting people on certain teams for purely political reasons—creating teams in name only.*

The dysfunctional nature of such teams can result in silo behavior, turf fights, and arguments over scarce resources. Its members may lack a holistic orientation and be unable to look at the organization in a more comprehensive way. After all, to be a constructive organizational participant necessitates that, at times, some functions will experience a restriction in resource allocation to benefit the whole organization. However, in some organizations it can be an uphill challenge to have the members of a dysfunctional team take a more holistic organizational view. Overcoming these situations can require considerable emotional intelligence. The most dangerous way of managing this process is to allow the most forceful individuals on the team to drive the choices concerning resource allocation.

A further obstruction to a well-functioning team is the power dynamics of succession. Should this come to the fore, every possible incumbent may become preoccupied in looking for ways to push his or her candidacy forward. As a result, a "zero-sum" game mindset could begin to dominate the psychological dynamics of the team. In such cases it is no wonder that "team killers" will raise their ugly head. There will be no collegiality, no collaboration, no coordination, and ultimately, no commitment.

> *In many dysfunctional teams it is noticeable that team members avoid dealing with conflict.*

What's noticeable in many of these dysfunctional teams is that team members avoid dealing with conflict. Instead, they resort to veiled discussions and guarded comments and there seems to be no buy-in to the decisions that are made. Given what we know of the darker side of teams, and in particular of a top executive team, resolving these problems can be a daunting challenge. Even so, as the decisions of such teams will have a great impact on the rest of the organization and its future, action needs to be taken to improve their modus operandi.

Leadership Group (Team) Coaching Comes to the Rescue

The challenge for executive coaches is to create teams where the members trust each other, and where there is a sense of commitment to decisions and action plans. We also aim to create a dynamic in which team members hold each other accountable and are able to focus on collective team results. If the organizational members possess this mindset, they can better understand how they can work together to achieve success for the organization.

As we have covered, with our extensive experience at facilitating the group dynamics that create more effective teams, we have gained extensive knowledge of how to tackle open or covert conflict and how to coach teams to excel in lateral communications and work within an organization to achieve greater levels of collaboration and better results.

> *All too often we encounter teams haunted by a dark cloud of distrust that needs to be prevented; trust can be seen as the glue that will keep a team together.*

The Trust Equation

An essential quality in creating high-performance teams is trust. All too often we encounter teams haunted by a dark cloud of distrust that needs to be prevented; trust can be seen as the glue that will keep a team together. Naturally, we recognize that trust will always be a delicate flower that easily wilts, and as the Greek philosopher Sophocles said, "trust dies, but distrust blossoms forth."[1] Clearly, the members of a team have to earn each other's trust, and experience has taught us that in many organizations this can be quite hard to obtain. Yet, if an organization wants to be high-performing, it will be essential to build trust.

We should add that from trust derive feelings of safety and security vis-à-vis the people who run the organization. Safety can be seen as the sanctuary where trust blossoms, and once established people will feel safe to speak their minds. Essentially, feelings of trust and safety will create a corporate culture where there will be constructive conflict resolution, greater commitment to

---

[1] Sophocles (401 BC/2014). "Oedipus at Colonus." In *The Theban Plays*. Trans. Peter J. Ahrensdorf and Thomas L. Pangle. Ithaca, NY and London: Cornell University Press, line 611.

the organization's objectives, and more accountability—all factors that translate into better results. Again, to create a culture of trust, we have learned that group coaching interventions can be second to none.

> *Feelings of trust and safety will create a corporate culture where there will be constructive conflict resolution, greater commitment to the organization's objectives, and more accountability.*

Creating "Aha" Experiences

From our work with thousands of senior executives, we have learned that once a boundary of trust has been established, people come to feel that even the most difficult issues can be resolved. However, in order for trust to blossom in organizational settings, covert issues need to become overt. The otherwise "undiscussables" need to be dealt with. This implies bringing otherwise repressed material into consciousness—an activity that may result in a great sense of emotional relief.

In our group coaching interventions to create more effective leadership teams, we need to address both overt and covert conflicts. To do so, we encourage the members of a team to speak up in various ways. It is important that they are heard. We have learned that the letting go of pent-up emotions through self-disclosure can be a cathartic first step. In fact, when the organizational participants are prepared to speak about knotty issues, they quickly discover that they aren't alone, and that others are experiencing very similar problems. From this "revelation," a vicarious learning process can be set into motion, which can be an extremely powerful experience. Having a better understanding of the source of possible conflicts may create "Aha!" or "Eureka!" moments—times when the members of the leadership team suddenly appear to find the answer to a riddle, or when seemingly out of the blue they understand the solution to whatever the problem is. As a result, it is like a light bulb switches on in their head. These moments are often referred to as tipping points: "signalling events" of great significance that contribute to meaningful life changes. A trusting group setting is the ideal place to encounter such tipping points.

> *A trusting group setting is the ideal place to encounter tipping points: "signalling events" of great significance that contribute to meaningful life changes.*

Catalysts of Change

In summary, the following forces tend to drive these moments of insight:

- The group setting provides a context for cathartic experiences. It allows executives to get things off their chest; to bring repressed feelings, fears, and covert conflicts to the surface which will help them to understand better why they do what they do.
- While listening to the life stories and challenges of other executives, the participants will come to realize that they are not alone in their confusion. Scientifically, the mirror neurons in their brain will respond to the actions they observe in others. This explains how we learn through mimicry, why we empathize with others, and how people learn how to model their behavior on that of other people.
- The process of mutual identification will be initiated, and the specific problems that have been shared will act to bring the team together, offering the opportunity to discuss jointly more effective ways of dealing with knotty issues at work.
- Bringing a psychodynamic-developmental lens into the discussion—i.e., applying the clinical paradigm—can set in motion a more extensive appraisal of why a leadership team has been doing things in a particular way. Understanding old patterns of interaction that once proved effective can help unpack dysfunctional behavior, thereby improving the chances for change.
- Such reflections can lead to a willingness to experiment in doing things differently—and, by doing so, create new opportunities in the future.
- Again, with regard to the mirroring process, the group setting offers the opportunity for vicarious learning. Executives come to realize that learning occurs not only through direct participation in dialogue but also through observing and listening to other people's stories.
- Executives going through the group coaching process often form a strong community. This feeling of social belonging also becomes a very powerful catalyst for change.

- The group setting is also an opportunity for collective learning. Explanation, clarification, and even direct advice about how to do things better can reduce anxiety and establish control when there is a troublesome issue. Executives can draw from their own rich experiences to share information about work issues and recommend different approaches.
- Finally, the altruistic motive behind the sharing of information can provide a further force for positive change. The desire to help others by offering support, reassurance, and insights can have a therapeutic effect, contributing to each executive's level of self-respect and well-being.

> *When executives are able to work together to improve their performance by finding more creative ways to deal with their professional environment, a positive contagion will infect the organization.*

Executive coaching is part of a holistic change process that can cultivate more effective and healthier organizations. When executives are able to work together to improve their performance by finding more creative ways to deal with their professional environment, a positive contagion will infect the organization. This contagion can spread hope and enthusiasm as the coaching culture supplants a formerly toxic or moribund environment. In other words, coaching interventions should also be viewed as iterative processes by which individuals can test and evaluate new behaviors in their daily life and adjust their actions until they feel that they have got it right. When done properly, executive coaching of leadership teams is a very dynamic process that can contribute to creativity and innovation in organizations; it can lead to the creation of more reflective, thoughtful executives.

Moreover, effective coaching in a group setting helps the members of a team to take control of their key team functions: setting direction, creating alignment throughout the organization, and building the commitment level of everyone needed to accomplish organizational objectives. Effective group coaching helps team members deal with questions such as the way the group gathers and synthesizes the information on which it bases its decisions. It makes these processes more overt.

Group coaching also yields economies of scale by leveraging time and resources. It provides group members with a sense of community and a safe forum in which to discuss the challenges they face and how they feel about them. This is especially important in enabling collaborative work in senior leadership teams, where the competitiveness of their members often makes it difficult to establish a climate that encourages adequate transparency.

Group coaching of a leadership team contributes to a deepened awareness of shared situations and provides the opportunity to learn from the experiences of others. Furthermore, it leads to an improved understanding of how an organization shares, processes, and uses information. Overall, effective group coaching of leadership teams can result in increased productivity through shared practices and lessons learned.

> *Coaching interventions should also be viewed as iterative processes by which individuals can test and evaluate new behaviors in their daily life and adjust their actions until they feel that they have got it right.*

The group coaching intervention technique creates an opportunity to receive and participate in coaching while also benefiting from the successes and challenges of the other group participants. When a participant supports and coaches other members of the group, they in turn gain increased self-mastery and leadership skills. Moreover, the intensity of the process creates a synergy of energy, commitment, and excitement. In contrast to individual coaching, wherein a person discusses the difficult relationships he or she has with various stakeholders, the center of attention in group coaching is those colleagues present in the room, and any overt or covert problems that come with their presence. The scalability of group coaching is important in making transformational change in organizations more likely.

Formulating a developmental action plan for every participant in the team—outlining what each member needs to work on, their responsibilities, and how these will contribute to the overall purpose of the business—ensures that each participant in a team coaching intervention has a stake in the learning plan of one another, all with the aim of the team accomplishing its set purpose.

> *We see group coaching of leadership teams as the "secret sauce" for enabling common people to arrive at uncommon results.*

However, it is also always important to be aware of the fact that making this kind of intervention successful will always entail certain unique complexities. To remain cognizant of these, an executive coach needs to maintain an aura of neutrality as a trusted advisor to *all* the members of the team. To help them metabolize their conflicted feelings, coaches act as a receptacle for the thoughts and emotions of each group member. At the same time, on occasion a coach may also need to give highly challenging feedback, encouraging the members of the team to think more broadly, yet still, in the role of coach, remaining focused on the wider interests of the organization. Despite all these difficulties, we see group coaching of leadership teams as the "secret sauce" for enabling common people to arrive at uncommon results.

7

The Leadership Audit

Give me a place to stand, and I will move the earth.
—*Archimedes*

Conversion is in its essence a normal adolescent phenomenon, incidental to the passage from the child's small universe to the wider intellectual and spiritual life of maturity.
—*William James*

It is the greatest of all mistakes to do nothing because you can only do a little. Do what you can.
—*Sydney Smith*

The Black Goat and the White Goat

For this explanation of a leadership audit, the fabulist Jean de la Fontaine[1] provides a moral story that is highly relevant to those who assess others. This story goes as follows:

> Once upon a time, in a certain forest, there lived a Black Goat and a White Goat. Although the forest was vast, in its center there was a wide chasm underneath which flowed a torrential river. The trunk of a fallen tree formed the only means of crossing the chasm, yet not even

---

[1] Jean de la Fontaine (1886/1668–1694). "The Two Goats." In *The Fables of La Fontaine*. Trans. Walter Thornbury. London and New York: Cassell, Petter, and Galpin.

two squirrels were able to pass each other in safety on this improvised bridge, which made the bravest animal tremble. But this was seemingly not so for our goats.

One day, as fate would have it, they both needed to cross the bridge. The Black Goat arrived on one side of the bridge, while the White Goat approached from the other. Both goats were determined to cross first, and an argument ensued with each goat unwilling to yield to the other.

As the dispute continued unresolved, the pair ended up butting heads with the other causing both goats to tumble off the bridge and into the torrent below.

The Instrumentation

Could this situation have been prevented? Would it have been possible to do something to prevent their idiotic behavior and instead lead the goats to a more sensible outcome?

A good place to start a group coaching intervention is by gaining a modicum of understanding of the psychology of the various members of a team. This means understanding how the team members interact with one another. Obviously, given the wide range of personalities that make up a team, we must assume from the outset that there will be many different ways in which they will relate to each other. Like the goats, all of us have different styles of working and communicating. Unfortunately, when we encounter people with a style that's different from our own, we may get frustrated with them and fail to recognize what they can contribute to the team.

> *A preliminary "audit" of the team dynamics is an opportunity for coaches to assess some of the critical issues in an organization.*

Consequently, a preliminary "audit" of the team dynamics is considered an opportunity for coaches to assess some of the critical issues in an organization. It is an opportunity to describe the various leadership styles of the members of the team, and to make an initial assessment of the organization's strengths and weaknesses. It can also be a chance to ascertain something of the organization's previously mentioned possible "undiscussables." The result of this careful preliminary questioning can be a valuable insight into the dos and don'ts of organizational life. It is also a point at which to ask what each individual would do if they were given the opportunity to make significant changes.

To achieve a greater insight into team dynamics at the initial stage of an intervention, personality and behavioral assessments can be great tools for improving a team's understanding of its own organizational culture. A discussion within the group-at-large of each member's leadership style will also give all participants a better understanding of why a person reacts to his or her colleagues in certain ways. It may help them to consider how they might relate to one another more effectively, understand that different approaches may be valid in different situations, and ultimately breed tolerance of individual team members.

> *Frequently, we note a considerable disparity between what leaders say they do, and what they really do.*

With a clinical lens, we have often observed that many senior executives need help to understand better how their behavior impedes effective functioning—both their own and that of others—within their organizations. Frequently, we note a considerable disparity between what leaders say they do, and what they really do. There will usually be many unconscious impediments to making changes. To help these people recognize blind spots, appropriate 360-degree feedback instrumentation can be a productive tool that enables them to compare their self-perceptions with the observations of their colleagues and others who know them well. We tell our clients to keep this statement in mind: "If one person tells you that you have ears like a donkey, ignore it. But if two people tell you so, get yourself a saddle." These assessments may provide them with a greater insight as to their "blind spots," which are often due to the psychological defenses that they are using.

To arrive at better reality testing we use a complete range of assessment instrumentation to help executives and teams function more effectively. Our developmental perspective involves diverse techniques such as **culture surveys, personality tests, leadership questionnaires, simulations, focus groups, individual interviews**, and **behavioral, more anthropological-like observations**. Together, these surveys allow us to give unique 360-degree feedback that can be used in a wide range of global contexts.

The 360-degree feedback instruments we use have been standardized based on the responses of tens of thousands of global, senior executives. They offer people a fully rounded picture of their personality and "inner theater," leadership style, and the culture of their organization. Among the instruments that we have developed are the Global Executive Leadership Inventory (GELI), the Global Executive Leadership Mirror (GELM), the Personality Audit (PA), the Leadership Archetypes Questionnaire (LAQ), and the Inner Theatre Inventory (ITI). For a more holistic, macro-organizational perspective, there is also the Organizational Culture Audit (OCA) that signals how different groups of people within the organization assess its culture.

> *However globalized organizations are, executives have very diverse world views and cultural values.*

In designing these various instruments, we have paid particular attention to the fact that, however globalized organizations are, executives have very diverse world views and cultural values. These instruments are all designed to reflect this and therefore need to have validity and relevance for many different cultures. In order to achieve this, the instruments were both psychometrically validated and tested on mixed cultural groups. Subsequently, they have been used in programs at numerous business schools and organizations around the world.

These individual, team, and organizational-oriented instruments inform interventions by deciphering personality characteristics, highlighting various leadership styles, uncovering team dynamics, and aiding the assessment of organizational culture. From experience, a side-by-side or team comparison of the results often helps participants in a group intervention (in particular, leadership teams) to understand better how personality traits affect leadership styles, the complementarities of roles, and the nature of the organization's culture. In turn, this helps participants to initiate change in manifest actions and behaviors, teams, and cultural understanding. This individual and team-oriented multi-party feedback can become the foundation of discussions about the organization's future.

With the assistance of this clinical instrumentation, well-informed group coaches can provide expertise on how to manage and develop executive teams and work with clients to implement a team leadership development process. They can help teams address such issues as gaining focus, aligning around a common purpose, discussing organizational values, clarifying roles, understanding different leadership styles (and their complementarities), resolving overt and covert conflict, improving business processes, managing change, understanding communication styles, and increasing productivity. They can also assist their clients in determining the gaps in their collective leadership skills and attributes. Lastly, they can help organizations to plan scenarios for the future, with the belief that, through teamwork, common people can achieve uncommon results.

> *Well-informed group coaches can help organizations to plan scenarios for the future, with the belief that, through teamwork, common people can achieve uncommon results.*

By returning to and discussing the results of these various instruments, executive coaches can help individuals to stay focused on what is essential to the success of the organization. They will be able to give clients developmental support and an honest evaluation of their strengths and weaknesses. This is a developmental process that needs to start from the top. Whatever the context, the involvement of those in senior positions will be crucial to the success of a coaching intervention. Setting an example and walking the talk—asking for feedback themselves and taking it seriously—are powerful symbolic gestures.

> *It is a fact of life that the further up the ladder an executive climbs, the less they may expect to receive honest feedback.*

Being Surrounded by Liars

Depending on the national and organizational culture, giving feedback can be difficult. For example, it is a fact of life that the further up the ladder an executive climbs, the less they may expect to receive honest feedback. In the context of superior–subordinate relationships, giving feedback can be difficult for many people. One consequence of this, as we mentioned before, is that many leaders find themselves in an echo chamber, isolated from reality by subordinates who are fearful of giving frank opinions. Sadly, fear is the bane of innovation and creativity. In organizations with extremely short-term reward structures, suspicion, power hoarding, and blame may all be part of the cultural DNA; where people are viewed as disposable goods, leadership coaching interventions may yield poor returns.

> *Fear is the bane of innovation and creativity ... and where people are viewed as disposable goods, leadership coaching interventions may yield poor returns.*

Creating an Effective Scenario

In our practice we use the 360-degree assessment tools listed above to initiate discussion about leadership development. As each person talks about some of the issues that he or she would like to reflect on with the help of the group, the other group members learn vicariously from the stories that are being told. Here, executives are engaged not only in a problem-solving exercise (in the form of action recommendations) but are also able to practice their leadership coaching skills with their peers. Using the Socratic approach—a way of interacting whereby the consultant asks the people he or she is working with open-ended questions to help them develop critical thinking skills—executives can learn what it means to listen actively, leading to greater understanding and thus aiding them in formulating their action plans. And when there is an ambiance of mutual respect, a sense of community grows, and participants realize that they are not alone in their confusion and from that can gain a sense of self-confidence.

We have observed that many executives have a lot to say about desired change but find, when it comes to acting, many of their good intentions evaporate. However, when discussion and discovery take place in a group setting (particularly with teams that need to work together) there is a greater possibility that individuals *will* act, as the other participants will have a stake in the individual's action plan. In this context, we encourage people to make what we call a "public declaration of intent": specifically, laying out two or three points to work on as part of their personal action plan for self-development. In addition, we ask them to select several people in their private or work life who can help them accomplish these goals. To add a sense of urgency, we may schedule one or more follow-up sessions several months later in which the person is asked to account for what has been accomplished. We sometimes say facetiously that our effectiveness is based on factors like shame and guilt, but also hope. After having made a public declaration of what they plan to do, the potential feelings of shame and guilt that would arise from breaking their promises help to keep the participants on track. Participants may be nervous or dubious of this approach, and yet public declarations of intent also create hope for a better future. Although we may also be called upon for one-to-one executive coaching or asked to make specific structural and/or strategic recommendations, we find that, in general, group coaching is extremely effective at fostering change at both the micro and macro level.

> *Virtual teams can function well and are here to stay, despite the added complexity of managing geography, time zones, and differences in culture, gender, age, and background.*

In addition, we have found that a group leadership coaching intervention can be an ideal way to create virtual teams that really work. What we have learned from the greatest social science experiment that has ever taken place—the Covid–19 pandemic—is that virtual teams can function well and are here to stay, despite the added complexity of managing geography, time zones, and differences in culture, gender, age, and background.

Of course, as with any other team, there will always be many overt and covert issues to be dealt with, but it goes without saying that tagging e-mails with emoticons will not solve problems. In effective teams (virtual or otherwise), people understand and respect one another; they are more inclined to see the other stakeholders' points of view; and they are more willing to collaborate. Our experience is that an initial face-to-face group intervention will be the starting point to create well-functioning virtual teams in boundaryless organizations, while also breaking patterns of silo-type behavior.

> *Tagging e-mails with emoticons will not solve problems.*

In the context of team coaching, knowledge management is another knotty issue that comes to the fore. This involves members of a team being prepared to exchange relevant information, thus creating an ambiance of trust between members, which will ultimately lead to a willingness to share. Clearly, to enable these kinds of interchanges requires far more than merely setting up a database of information and, similar to other problematic issues, failed knowledge-sharing initiatives can often be traced to a missing ingredient: trust. People will only share information if they feel comfortable with each other. They need to believe that their hard-won knowledge will not be hoarded somewhere but will be treated as a resource for the whole organization. As teams work together in a group coaching setting, they can discuss and reach agreements on fair processes for sharing knowledge, and also for giving credit where credit is due. And of course, the capacity to build effective knowledge-sharing systems gives an organization an enormous competitive advantage.

When executive coaching is applied to teams, it leads to a more egalitarian, high-trust interface that transcends traditional superior–subordinate relationships. The fundamental premise in the group coaching process of a team is that all members of the team develop a genuine realization that "we're all working for the same company." This again breaks silo-like behavior.

> *The fundamental premise in the group coaching process of a team is that all members of the team develop a genuine realization that "we're all working for the same company."*

Furthermore, group coaching a team not only supports and enables the realization of a team's performance potential but also increases its capacity for self-sustained development. When a team is operating at full capacity, everybody pulls their weight and is accountable for their contribution to the team performance.

In addition, we have found that group coaching a team is strongly recommended for teams going through a significant change process, such as adapting to a new CEO, as well as being ideal for new teams that are under pressure to show results quickly. Highly successful teams engage in both individual and team coaching, addressing issues specific to an individual and broader global issues relating to the team. This may include team development with a specific focus on critical issues, vision, mission, goals, roles, corporate culture, team support, and leadership development. The benefits of group coaching a team, as indicated by clients, are summarized in the box below.

The Benefits of Group Coaching Teams as Indicated by Clients
Group coaching of teams can help a team to:

- Clarify its goals, identify obstacles to change, explore options, and develop appropriate action plans
- Identify the characteristics of effective teams
- Understand the barriers to performance that are hindering the team
- Create a better appreciation of the team's strengths and challenges
- Increase the team's capacity to arrive achieve high performance

- Align individual performance with team goals
- Understand better the dynamics within the team
- Arrive at more effective team decision-making
- Identify the roles each member of the team plays
- Identify overt and covert conflict within the team
- Manage conflict when it arises
- Assist "assimilation coaching," when new members are introduced to a functioning team
- Communicate more effectively
- Develop fully into a more cohesive, trusting, collaborative unit
- Develop more effective leadership skills within the team
- Take advantage of peer coaching in a team setting
- Align team norms with an accountability structure
- Assure that individual and team accountability structures are built into every task and project
- Navigate a period of significant change and transition
- Deal with virtual and cross-functional team challenges
- Ensure that feedback, brainstorming, and challenging beliefs become an acceptable practice between team members
- Create self-organizing teams
- Maximize and leverage the strengths of a team
- Set the ground rules and logistics of team processes (for example: How often will the team meet? Where will the meetings take place? What are the rules for the running of meetings? What arbitration procedure will take place when the team cannot come to an agreement?)
- Engage in regular process review meetings and assess how successful the team meetings have been.

One individual can only do so much, but as a group the sky is the limit. All the members of the group will rise when they are prepared to lift each other.

With Unity Comes Strength

We are very aware of the fact that change is seldom achieved by one person; more often than not, amazing things happen when like-minded people are committed to a singular goal. In any group situation, we always keep in mind that one individual can only do so much, but as a group the sky is the limit. All the members of the group will rise when they are prepared to lift each other. As has also been made clear, teamwork can be challenging at times. We recognize and here reiterate the delicacy of trust within a group of people, and the ease with which it can be destroyed. However, if people are prepared to choose forgiveness over bitterness and to collaborate over the pursuit of personal goals, much can be achieved. Clearly, effective change will be impossible if not everybody is willing to collaborate and cooperate. The mantra of this chapter is that unity provides strength.

> *If people are prepared to choose forgiveness over bitterness and to collaborate over the pursuit of personal goals, much can be achieved.*

8

The Three Mental Triangles

Philosophy [Nature] is written … in mathematical language, and the characters are triangles, circles, and other geometric figures, without which means it is humanly impossible to understand a word of it; without these it is a wandering in vain through a dark labyrinth.
—Galileo Galilei

If the triangles were to make a God, they would give him three sides.
—de Montesquieu

Above all, the search after truth and its eager pursuit are peculiar to man. And so, when we have leisure from the demands of business cares, we are eager to see, to hear, to learn something new, and we esteem a desire to know the secrets or wonders of creation as indispensable to a happy life. Thus we come to understand that what is true, simple, and genuine appeals most strongly to a man's nature.
—Marcus Tullius Cicero

The Traveler and the Wise Man

There is a Sufi tale of a traveler who came to the city seeking advice. "I'm looking for the wisest man to advise me!" he said to the person in charge of the city gate.

The guard pointed to a disheveled old man who was playing marbles with some street-urchins. "You might give him a try," he replied.

The traveler approached the strange-looking man and, much to his surprise, he received excellent advice.

"Thank you!" said the traveler. "But I don't understand: with all your wisdom, why are you just playing marbles with children?"

"They wanted me to be in charge of the city," the man explained, "playing the fool was the only way to escape!"

The Triangle of Mental Life

As human relationships can be quite complex, at times it has been quite useful to ask what seem to be foolish questions. Taking on the role of the fool, but akin to the kind of fool in Shakespeare's King Lear—the morosoph or wise fool—can be very enlightening. We have found that such a "fool," in playing the role of mediator between leader and followers, can bring to the surface many conflictual themes. Taking on this role has provided us with many insights that otherwise would not have been that evident.

An issue that often arises during the process of helping people change, be it in an individual or group setting, is the question of what kind of interpersonal psychological dynamics are at play. What's *really* going on? Something we have found to be helpful as a conceptual tool for explaining these dynamics is the use of various intrapersonal and interpersonal triangles.

The most basic, the "Triangle of Mental Life," illustrates how thoughts (cognition), feelings/emotions (affect), and behaviors are interconnected and together shape our experiences and reactions to different situations. The three elements of this triangle are inextricably linked and influence each other in a continuous feedback loop (see Fig. 8.1).

The cognitive aspect of the triangle encompasses the various **thoughts** that continually run through our mind, both those we are aware of and those more latent. Naturally, these thoughts present themselves or are expressed in various ways: in a verbal form such as with words, sentences, and explicit ideas, as well as in a non-verbal way in the form of mental images. These thoughts can be positive or negative. Often, negative thoughts are the product of cognitive distortions. Good examples of cognitive distortions are all-or-nothing thinking, making overgeneralizations, discounting the positive, jumping to conclusions, or thinking with "should," "must," and "ought" statements. In other words, the cognitive aspect of the triangle reflects how we make sense of situations and the running commentary that takes place in our minds throughout our lives.

Emotions are another integral part of this triangle of mental life, and refer to the way we *feel* in response to our thoughts. By recognizing how thoughts directly impact our feelings, we obtain greater insight as to our emotional responses. For instance, when we get angry, we may feel our face flushing.

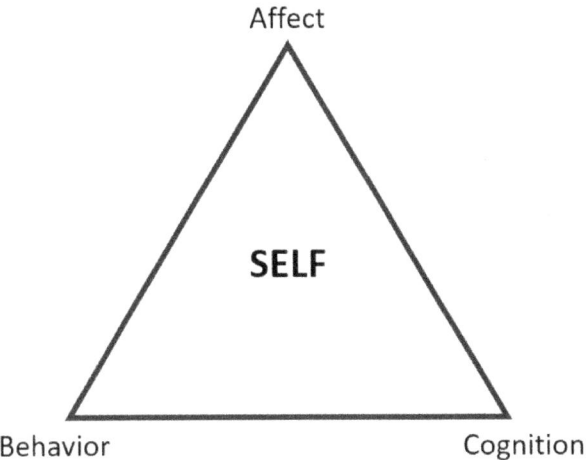

Fig. 8.1 Triangle of Mental Life

When we suffer anxiety, we may feel our heart pounding and muscles tensing. And these real physical feelings can become problematic when we fail to deal with them in a situation-appropriate manner.

The third and final component of the triangle pertains to our ***behavioral*** responses. It is concerned with how we respond to stimuli and the things we do or don't do as a result. Behavior encompasses both outward actions—such as how we interact with others or engage in activities—and internal responses such as avoidance, procrastination, or rumination. By acknowledging the connection between thoughts, feelings, and actions we can identify how our own thoughts and emotions drive our behavior. Moreover, we can develop greater self-control and make more intentional choices as to how we act.

> *By acknowledging the connection between thoughts, feelings, and actions we can identify how our own thoughts and emotions drive our behavior. Moreover, we can develop greater self-control and make more intentional choices as to how we act.*

The Triangle of Conflict

With the same triangular format as the cognitive model, we also refer to the "Triangle of Conflict." This triangle illustrates the tension between what we desire and the consequences of fulfilling those desires. Here our core emotions come into play, but so too do our imagined consequences if we were to act out these desires (see Fig. 8.2).

Humans are hardwired to experience core emotions such as sadness, fear, anger, joy, excitement, and disgust in certain environments which, when activated, trigger a host of associated physiological reactions that prime us for action. Simultaneously, however, feelings such as shame, anxiety, and guilt may also come to the fore and try to block these primitive emotional reactions. Various defensive reactions therefore emerge as a means of managing these core emotions.

To sum up, the triangle of conflict illustrates the following tensions: we may desire something (impulse/feelings) and this desire may or may not be fulfilled depending on a host of factors that are perhaps out of our control. An unacceptable desire, however, will stimulate fear (anxiety/conflict) and consequently result in various defense reactions that can manifest in negative or dysfunctional behavior (defensive/maladaptive behavior patterns)—behavior that acts as a block to our awareness of unpleasant thoughts or feelings.

Fig. 8.2 Triangle of Conflict

> *Our task as psychological detectives is to find out what underlying emotions our clients are defending themselves against.*

Our task as psychological detectives is to find out what underlying emotions our clients are defending themselves against. What is the nature of the underlying feelings that drive each individual's actions? What's really going on that is resulting in such unhelpful behavior? To obtain a better grasp of underlying emotions, we ask a number of clarifying questions to establish why someone is behaving in what appears to be a dysfunctional manner. In an individual or group setting, clarification through open questioning can result in a greater specificity of the problem. If done well, the problem will be made more explicit and, if recognizable, the defensive reactions are pointed out. Are these defenses of a more primitive nature, like splitting (envisaging that the world is divided into people who are perceived as "good" or "bad") and projection (a process whereby people attribute or recognize their own thoughts and feelings as those of others), or are they more sophisticated, such as the use of intellectualization or humor? Subsequently, the person who is in the "hot seat"—meaning the individual who is being addressed—will gain a better grasp of his or her situation.

One illustration of this occurred in a group intervention centered around a particular female CEO. Here, the other participants asked her to clarify the nature of her relationships with other women. The members of the group also prompted her to tell them something about her daughter—a relationship that she had in previous discussions explained as being quite difficult. Given the nature of this conflicted relationship, she was also asked questions about her mood management: why did she often get so angry when dealing with other people? And what did she think were the reasons for her outbursts of anger, in particular with women?

In the case of this female CEO, we can explore her behavior and try to explain it through the triangle of conflict. One underlying issue had to do with her anger toward her mother. At times when she felt that her mother was being unreasonable when she was growing up, she had felt like "she could kill her." Of course, given the level of dependence a child has on her mother, to express that thought (as a very small child) would have been a very conflict-ridden proposition. The thought alone would cause an enormous amount of anxiety, and her defense mechanism was to repress these angry thoughts such that they were out of her conscious awareness. In addition to this, she admitted feeling angry at her father for not standing up for her and, again, her defensive structure was to deny those emotions and instead pretend that everything was all right.

What also emerged from this discussion was that as well as using repression, she used another defense mechanism called displacement. This means she redirected her angry feelings toward people who were less "dangerous" or less emotionally significant than her mother. Here her "victims" were her daughter, sisters, girlfriends, and, later, husbands and colleagues. Furthermore, it also appeared that she suffered from conversion symptoms (implying that psychic conflicts transformed into somatic symptoms) in the form of migraine headaches.

The associations made by the members of the group following her presentation laid the groundwork for a thoughtful, detailed reappraisal of why this CEO was behaving the way she did and was prone to irrational outbursts of anger. Thanks to the discussion, she obtained greater clarity about the nature of her reactions toward other people. Most importantly, she came to understand the dysfunctionality of her defenses and became aware of the inappropriateness of her angry outbursts. She became more conscious of the ways she dealt with her feelings and arrived at a number of powerful insights about herself. It became quite clear that these insights about the root causes of her behavior were quite painful, but after internalizing this information, she began to experiment with different ways of interacting with others.

The way the core issue was selected and the group reached out to her was an experience that, to date, she had probably never had. However, the support she received when she (with the help of the other members of the group) tried to unravel her conflicted relationships made her feel deeply understood, not only concerning her current difficulties but also in her long-standing sense of not feeling completely appreciated. That the group showed a deep, nonjudgmental understanding of why she had been behaving in a certain way made her feel truly supported, and subsequently it encouraged her to work more on herself.

The Triangle of Relationships

What adds a deeper dimension to what's going on below the surface is another structure we refer to as the "Triangle of Relationships." This concerns the important role that transferential relationships play in an interpersonal setting. What this triangle points out—and was exemplified in the example of the female CEO given in the previous section—is that in every situation there are two kinds of relationships. First, there is the "real" relationship between

Fig. 8.3 Triangle of Relationships

a person and others. This real relationship however becomes the background or context for a second kind of relationship: the transference relationship (see Fig. 8.3).

Basically, transference is a phenomenon in which we direct feelings or desires relating to important figures in our life—such as our primary caretakers—toward other people. It occurs when our brain tries to comprehend a current experience by examining the present through the lens of the past. To some extent all relationships are colored by previous relationships, and inevitably the relationships that have the most lasting potency and which color almost every subsequent encounter are those that we had with our earliest caretakers.

> *Transference occurs when our brain tries to comprehend a current experience by examining the present through the lens of the past.*

Much of our behavior in a contemporary setting will have its roots in these privileged relationships with early caretakers. As we relive those earlier, primary relationships again and again, stereotypical (almost automatic) behavior patterns emerge. That is, we tend to repeat behavioral patterns that we used with important people from our past, relating to others in the way we may have related to our parents as children, yet on some level forgetting that we are now adults. In other words, we seem to become unconsciously confused as to person, time, and place, which suggests that these past relationships have become organizing themes within our personality structure. Attitudes, thoughts, and emotional responses have emerged that are currently maladaptive and relate directly to interpersonal processes that were prevalent in earlier times.

> *We tend to repeat behavioral patterns that we used with important people from our past, relating to others in the way we may have related to our parents as children, yet on some level forgetting that we are now adults.*

In a group intervention, the triangle of relationships can provide a conceptual structure for assessing patterns of response, pointing out similarities between past relationships and how we interact in the present. Thus, anyone hoping to make sense of interpersonal encounters needs to understand these transferential processes.

Linking the Past with the Present

In our work with executives we have discovered (like many psychotherapists and coaches have before us) that these transferential observations can be a major tool in helping people change. Understanding these old patterns of interaction becomes important in recognizing similarities with ongoing specific behavioral patterns that are no longer helpful. Making clients aware of these patterns can be a powerful "aha" experience—their personal lightbulb moment.

When meaningful links can be established between present relationships and those of the distant past, the process of changing the way we deal with life situations is more likely to be successful. By changing the long-standing and repetitive transference of maladaptive past patterns onto current relationships, a person's style of interacting will be changed. Therefore, by using ourselves as an instrument in our interactions with our clients, we can reflect on the patterns that we observe and provide greater insight as to their origins.

> *When meaningful links can be established between present relationships and those of the distant past, the process of changing the way we deal with life situations is more likely to be successful.*

Returning to the example of our female CEO, the facilitators and the other participants in the group pointed out similarities between her relationship with her mother and the way she interacted with the female executives at the office (and also toward us)—a comparison that she found quite helpful. It also clarified her conflicted relationship with her daughter. What contributed to this was the fact that, several times during the group intervention session, she experienced these seemingly irrational outbursts of anger to what appeared to be innocuous comments. What she came to understand during the group process was the transferential nature of these outbursts. The underlying theme for this angry lashing out could be articulated as her saying: "you are a 'bad' mother, you don't really care about how I feel." Another theme emerged from the memory of her father's behavior: "men are weak, why don't you stand up for me when I am wronged?" Both themes were made more explicable to the participants by her description of her early life experiences. This became all the more explicit when she snapped at one of the female executives during the group intervention for no apparent reason. When members of the group pointed out the connection, she came to recognize the dysfunctional behavior patterns that had become her deep-seated defensive response and she realized that what may have been survival behavior when she was younger, was no longer functional or appropriate in her adult self.

Gradually, the support, validation, and the provision of safe and encouraging relationships with members of the group became crucial to her inner journey toward self-understanding. The feeling that other people *did* care, and the empathy expressed by others, seemed to make a real difference. What really touched her was the way that the group reached out and seemed to be truly concerned. They listened to her story in a non-judgmental way and accepted her with all her frailties.

> *One of the important tasks of a change catalyst is to decipher what the client is trying to enact.*

As she began to recognize the connections between past and present, her resistance to change became weaker. Increasingly, she was prepared to make small changes in her life and, little by little, she became mentally prepared to adopt more constructive patterns of behavior. Hence, what we can learn from this example is that one of the important tasks of a change catalyst is to decipher what the client is trying to enact. The ensuing challenge is to help the client prevent themselves from acting out the usual script, and instead embark on a new, more constructive one.

Fig. 8.4 The Three Triangles of Insight

Restructuring a Person's Inner Theater

From a conceptual point of view, these three triangles (the Triangle of Mental Life, the Triangle of Conflict, and the Triangle of Relationships) have been presented with a view to clarifying the psychological dynamics of the change process. In applying the insights derived from these triangles, pressure can be exerted upon the person who is embarking on a change process from a number of different fronts. These fronts will be **affect restructuring**, **defense restructuring**, and **self-perception restructuring**. These interwoven forces make up the core of a person's personality and must therefore be dealt with in order to drive personal change (see Fig. 8.4 for the three triangles of insight.)

With this awareness of the three triangles, we always keep a number of questions in mind when explaining and exploring our clients' behavioral patterns:

- What behavioral observations can be made? Is their behavior appropriate to the situation that they find themselves in?
- What kind of emotions do they use? Could they express these emotions more effectively?
- What habitual defenses do they use to deal with stressful situations? Are there certain patterns that they can recognize? Is there anything that should be changed about these defenses?
- How do they perceive themselves? Do they feel secure about who they are? What do they think others think about them? Are they capable of honest self-appraisal?

As we have seen, these questions may be difficult to answer alone. Often, individuals need help from others in order to obtain answers. Change requires a person to relinquish defenses (**defense restructuring**), express emotions honestly (**affect/emotional restructuring**), and perceive themselves and others in ways that accord with reality (**self-perception restructuring**). They may also require the support of others in dealing with the sense of loss that comes with every change effort.

> *Change requires a person to relinquish defenses, express emotions honestly, and perceive themselves and others in ways that accord with reality.*

These three triangles of insight are integral to all of our work and our more clinical approach. For example, taking the triangle of conflict in the case of the female CEO, it didn't take too much time to identify her use of specific defenses. Repression, denial, projection, and conversion were all recognizable in her personal repertoire of behavior. She also tended to deny responsibility for some of her actions; i.e., she would forget certain things (usually the more unpleasant things she had to do). In addition, as we have already mentioned, she had the tendency to redirect angry feelings toward others and, when under stress, demonstrated conversion symptoms in the form of incapacitating migraines.

If we now consider the triangle of relationships, as her case has illustrated, the problem is that although many of her behavioral patterns may have been quite adaptive in the context where they were first learned, they had now become maladaptive. As a result, she would sometimes become "confused" in time and place when dealing with people, acting out old behavior patterns that were no longer appropriate in the present.

> *There exists a natural human tendency to achieve gratification by means learned in the past.*

Returning to the triangle of conflict, in this example the CEO's defensive structure, denial of responsibility, and forgetting were successful survival mechanisms in her family, and physical problems such as migraines were her attempt to get some attention from her father. What her behavior demonstrates is that there exists a natural human tendency to achieve gratification by means learned in the past. Whereas previously, these defenses may have been quite effective, as solutions in adult life they are no longer good enough and contribute to dysfunctional behavior patterns that are now negative. In order to change (here defense restructuring), however, people such as the female CEO in our example first need to recognize this defensive behavior, then understand its origin, and ultimately build better alternative coping mechanisms. This person would be better off if she becomes aware of the costs and benefits of the way she uses her defense. That is, what does it mean to give up certain defenses? Are there other ways of dealing with the vicissitudes of life? What is the best way to go about it? Only after recognition will people be able to relinquish these now dysfunctional defensive reactions.

> *Some people believe that* not *thinking about a conflicted issue will make them feel better than thinking about it.*

In a group session, our female CEO described an incident where she publicly humiliated someone due to an error that they had made. During the workshop, she was asked several questions pertaining to this disastrous interaction: "Did it work?" "Have you found that not thinking about this issue made you feel better?" "Do you think that you were effective by not apologizing for this incident?" "Could you have handled the situation in a different way?"

Some people believe that *not* thinking about a conflicted issue will make them feel better than thinking about it, and this use of denial as a defense can, at times, be very adaptive. In such cases, it would be hard to change such a behavior pattern. However, in our example, our client's prominent position in the company meant that her behavior had become counterproductive and she had come to realize that acting in an inappropriate manner, and then behaving as if nothing had happened, was not useful or acceptable.

> *The inability to express emotions interpersonally can have dire consequences.*

Another aspect of personality change concerns recognizing how a person experiences and expresses emotions. The inability to express emotions interpersonally can have dire consequences. In emotional/affect restructuring we have to explore verbal, non-verbal, physiological, and action tendencies in fantasy. Emotional reactions can be both within and outside of our awareness; they can be labeled or remain unknown. All these variations on a theme necessitate being extremely observant. We have to repeatedly ask ourselves a set of questions: What kind of emotions do certain situations evoke? Do certain types of emotional reactions lead to conflict? How do we feel physically when expressing a certain emotion? Are there other ways of expressing emotions? Is it possible to role-play certain difficult emotional situations?

In the context of emotions, another question that could be posed to someone like our CEO is whether she believed that her use of anger has the desired results. She could have said: "That's the way I am. I can't change how I act." Yet, the last time she had a public outburst of anger, the person who was the object of her wrath left the organization and her behavior had thus led to the loss of a valuable employee. However, after the workshop, she came to understand that a more constructive way of handling anger was for her to reflect on the way she was dealing with other people. She saw that, given her prominent position in the company, public displays of anger would frighten others and damage overall morale. The group discussion made her realize that although it was acceptable to be angry, it needed to be channeled in a more constructive manner. Her new awareness of how her emotional outbursts affected others formed a significant step in her journey toward change.

> *The process of organizing experiences into habitual patterns of expectation starts at infancy and informs our future interactions with others that are likely to be self-confirming.*

Another area of change we encounter is that of self-perception, particularly how we can restructure our sense of self-esteem and self-image (self-perception restructuring). Over time, people seem to develop habitual patterns or theories to process information on how they expect others to respond to them. This process of organizing experiences into habitual patterns of expectation starts at infancy and informs our future interactions with others that are likely to be self-confirming. The child who is treated with empathic respect and understanding is likely to grow up into an adult who likes him or herself, enjoys human interaction, and will have few difficulties in establishing supportive relationships. In contrast, the mistreated child will understand relationships in unhelpful ways, and come to behave in a manner that can become a self-fulfilling prophecy. In short, the way we construct reality tends to create the reality that we confront. However, having a negative sense of how others perceive us and how we view others can lead to serious interpersonal problems. To stop this dysfunctional perception of ourselves taking root, we have to find the origin of this feeling. Adaptive and maladaptive inner representations need to be identified, after which a process of self-affirmation is required to rebuild our perception of ourselves and of others. Creating a more positive and realistic perception of ourselves, however, is not easy to do alone. Often, we need the help of others, and, in an individual or group setting, these adaptive or maladaptive inner representations of self and others can be identified and addressed. Subsequently, efforts can be made to alter the perception of the self through exposure and the care of others.

> *In short, the way we construct reality tends to create the reality that we confront.*

In our example, it proved beneficial to point out to her that in her relationship with men she was engaged in a self-fulfilling prophecy: because she perceived herself as not being likable, she created situations that made her unlikable. Her two failed marriages were a living proof of this. She admitted that, while married, she felt compelled to pick fights with her husbands as though testing their attachment to her—to the point that they would leave her. Consequently, each time, this behavior acted to confirm her belief that she was unloved.

Hence, the challenge in this case was to change the CEO's perception of not being loveable. Simply recognizing this pattern in her behavior was a major step toward change. The next challenge was to trust and accept other people's views that she could be likable. Thus, she needed to use her defenses more constructively and to find more appropriate ways of dealing with her temper. In fact, improving her relationships with people at work was further progress, and it indicated that she was capable of establishing new or more meaningful relationships, whether with her colleagues, daughter, or a significant other.

> *Mental strength isn't about avoiding hardships, it's about facing them head-on, persevering, and looking for ways to grow from them. Even if we don't have the power to choose where we came from, we can choose where we go next.*

Lastly, mental well-being for this female CEO meant appreciating her abilities, working productively, coping with the normal stresses of life, and making positive contributions to her community. To emerge from her defensive cocoon she needed to recognize how much she had to offer to others. Thus, as our example illustrates, mental strength isn't about avoiding hardships, it's about facing them head-on, persevering, and looking for ways to grow from them. Even if we don't have the power to choose where we came from, we can choose where we go next. In this respect, self-care and self-compassion, difficult as they may be, should always be a priority.

9

Deconstructing the Individual Change Process

Only the supremely wise and the most deeply ignorant do not alter.
—Confucius

If we could change ourselves, the tendencies in the world would also change. As a man changes his own nature, so does the attitude of the world change towards him.
—Mahatma Gandhi

If you want to make enemies, try to change something.
—Woodrow Wilson

The Pike's Dilemma

In this allegory there was an enormous pike that lived in a large aquarium divided into two parts. In one section there was the pike, and in the other lived numerous minnows. When the carnivorous pike was first put in the aquarium, it made a frantic effort to get at the minnows, but every time it tried to reach them it simply hit the glass. Eventually, the pike gave up, realizing that it was impossible. When the glass partition was removed, the pike continued to ignore the minnows. The pike had learnt a specific behavior pattern which it seemingly could not unlearn.

As the previous chapters have suggested, change is not easy. People tend to hold on to dysfunctional patterns, however illogical they may appear to others, and cannot seem to change their perspective on life without expending a great deal of effort. It has also been noted that the reason why people cling so tenaciously to the status quo is not always easy to determine as there are many conscious and unconscious obstacles on the path toward change. Yet, in this age of discontinuity, it has become clear that the organizations that survive and grow through the decades are those that can respond effectively to the changing demands of their environment.

> *In this age of discontinuity, it has become clear that the organizations that survive and grow through the decades are those that can respond effectively to the changing demands of their environment.*

This leads us back to the question of how executive coaches and consultants can help organizational leaders proactively to drive the process of change. How can they become most effective as change agents? How can they apply their knowledge of the dynamics of personal transformation to their lives and work? Now that change has become the rule rather than the exception, these questions are critical to corporate survival and success.

In the previous chapter we discussed the three different triangles of insight (see Fig. 8.4) as models for individual change, and we can see how these are equally integral to the process of organizational change and transformation. Without a change in people's mindsets, it will be difficult to execute an organizational change process. Because organizations are made up of collections of people, the successful implementation of organizational change will require an understanding of individual responses to the process. A lack of attention to the personal experiences of those in an organization—whether this is consciously or unconsciously—will hugely hinder the process, and the effort may well go down as yet another failed change attempt. For this reason, change agents interested in organizational transformation need to begin by actively learning about the various transformative stages that make up individual change.

> *Individual and organizational change processes cannot exist without the other. Thoughtful change agents must recognize this interdependence if they hope to induce, facilitate, and even accelerate what can otherwise be a hugely lengthy intervention.*

Giving consideration to the underlying dynamics and following a more clinical approach can turn the potential for organizational transformation into a more realistic endeavor. In short, individual and organizational change processes cannot exist without the other. Thoughtful change agents must recognize this interdependence if they hope to induce, facilitate, and even accelerate what can otherwise be a hugely lengthy intervention.

Banging Your Head Against a Brick Wall

In the early days, as consultants and coaches, we started out by delivering lengthy lectures, explaining to executives the error of their ways and the poor decisions that caused their organizations to malfunction. We would spend time ascertaining what and why change was necessary. In fact, we applied every kind of logic in a bid to explain why their efforts were unsustainable. Although these observations may have made intellectual sense, simply pointing them out didn't make an iota of difference. Most of these executives paid merely lip service to our harangues, agreed with what we had to say, but merrily kept on doing the same thing they always had. Eventually, we realized that it was unproductive to continue banging our heads against a wall. Logic alone was not good enough—we ourselves needed to change our approach if we were to reach these people. We needed to practice what we preached.

During a group intervention, one of the executives received a considerable amount of feedback from the other participants and faculty about his tendency to remain emotionally aloof in difficult situations. He used distancing as a defensive mechanism and, when stressed, he would just withdraw and not react. It was highly likely that he had heard comments before about his irritating behavior and was cognitively aware of the problem. This knowledge alone however was not sufficient enough to make him change how he dealt with other people—more "ammunition" was needed. The question became what could be done to get a "hook" into him? What could we do that would make a real difference?

As part of our 360-degree feedback exercise, we decided to gather information about him from people who were both important and emotionally close to him. During the second phase of this workshop, we presented him with this feedback, not only from the people at the office (the more traditional way to get a better handle on a person's leadership style), but also from close friends, his wife, children, and other family members. This time we could see that the feedback had made a real impact on him. What was especially poignant was a very emotional statement from his 19-year-old daughter (family members and friends had responded to an e-mail that asked questions as to how they perceived him, and what he should change about his behavior). With teary eyes (very unusual for an otherwise very composed banker) he shared a note from his daughter in which she expressed her sadness at his inapproachability, and her enduring and frustrated wish to be closer to him. She referred to all the efforts she had made in the past to do so and how she had wanted a real relationship.

This note was a turning point. From that moment onward the other participants noticed a change in his behavior. He became truly emotionally involved in the discussions that took place at the workshop and listened to the insights provided by the other participants. With this new openness, the other presentations began to touch him emotionally too. Most importantly, however, was that he began to experiment with other ways of behaving when in stressful situations. That isn't to say that there were no lapses, but if at times he fell back into his old patterns of behavior, the comments of the other participants were there, reminding him of the feedback from his daughter. The other participants functioned as a "learning/coaching community" to reinforce the positives of emotional availability. Gradually, over the course of half a year, his new, more expressive behavior became second nature to him.

This specific incident helped us to look at personal change processes in a different manner, one which extended the role of individual executive coaching helping the group dynamics. It illustrated the power that various constituencies can have in furthering the change effort. By gathering insights from a wider social sphere—both at home, the office, and the newly established learning/coaching community of peers—all parties had a stake in his change effort, reinforcing the value of being open to approaching situations in different ways.

> *One of the main obstacles the individual, and therefore also the organization, may encounter in the processes we instigate, is the strong opposition to change prevalent in all social beings.*

The Stages of Individual Change

One of the main obstacles the individual, and therefore also the organization, may encounter in the processes we instigate, is the strong opposition to change prevalent in all social beings. This instinctive force represents the high levels of anxiety we associate with the uncertainty of, for example, engaging in something new, or finding ourselves exposed to old dangers and risks. In an effort to reduce such anxiety, people resort naturally to avoidant patterns of behavior—sheltering themselves from frightening situations—which become deeply ingrained. Repeating past behavior, in spite of the problems it may cause, is an all too human, often rather self-destructive attempt to take control of traumatic situations. Equally, a fear of acknowledging that the present situation is not sustainable or good enough can cause us to freeze. Ironically, in many instances we seem to favor the painful but familiar to the promising but unknown. As a consequence, people are often willing to endure extremely unsatisfactory situations rather than take steps to improve things. Indeed, behind each individual's adherence to the status quo lie complex, often unconscious processes, most of which serve a protective purpose. Some people may also resist change partly because of the "secondary gain"—the psychological benefits, such as sympathy and attention, that their dysfunctional behavior may illicit from others.

> *Repeating past behavior, in spite of the problems it may cause, is an all too human, often rather self-destructive attempt to take control of traumatic situations … in many instances we seem to favor the painful but familiar to the promising but unknown.*

Prerequisites of Personal Change

During our work attempting to facilitate personal change, we have found there to be a number of prerequisites: the role of negative emotions, the focal event, and the public declaration of intent (see Chapter 7). Each of these prerequisites plays an important role in activating and sustaining the process of personal transformation. These are the preliminary steps that are necessary for the internalization of personal change and over the years we have observed there to be a certain sequence to this process.

Step 1: Negative Emotions

If the human tendency is to *resist* change, how does the process of change ever get underway? Why does a person's resistance start to weaken? Given the relative stability of personality, setting the process of change in motion requires a strong inducement which may come in the form of pain or distress. In short, discomfort needs to outweigh the comfort of remaining with the status quo if it is to act as a catalyst for change.

Studies of personal change indicate that a high level of stress is a major inducement to change. Stressors may come in the form of family tensions, health problems, negative social situations, accidents, feelings of isolation that can easily lead to a sense of helplessness and insecurity, problematic behavior, distressing incidents happening to someone close, not to mention the other day-to-day hassles and frustrations of life. Those of our clients who considered themselves to have changed often describe having experienced high levels of unpleasant emotions—for example, anxiety, anger, sadness, or frustration—in the period prior to their major change efforts, most precipitated by stressors such as those listed above. The intensity of their negative emotions made them more profoundly aware of the potentially serious consequences of perpetuating their dysfunctional behavior patterns. In fact, individuals who reported a major change said that they had reached a point where their habitual behavior was increasingly difficult to sustain; they had become locked into cycles that were destructive to their psychological well-being. Their negative emotions—and the consequences they anticipated if those emotions continued—forced them into weighing up the pros and cons (not necessarily a conscious process) of the existing problem in seeking a solution. They recalled feeling that something had to change dramatically to break their negative cycles and personal stalemate.

> *Discomfort needs to outweigh the comfort of remaining with the status quo if it is to act as a catalyst for change.*

In many cases these people realized that their "bad days" had turned into a bad year—the isolated or occasional periods of discontent had changed progressively into a near constant unhappiness—and they were no longer able to deny the need for change.

This might be considered as a "crystallization" of discontent, as they recognized their feelings were part of a greater pattern of unhappiness. Identifying a general pattern made their problem into a coherent entity, compounded to create a new perspective of their situation. Many people then reported having a point of realization—what might be considered an "aha!" moment of clarity—when they were finally able to achieve a more objective assessment of their problem. For the first time they saw clearly that neither the passage of time nor minor changes in behavior would improve the situation—indeed, the situation was only likely to deteriorate further if they did not take more drastic action.

This insight into the significant measures required to improve the situation did not always compel these people to act automatically. However, it usually sets in motion a willingness to consider alternatives to the adverse situation. When people finally made the transition from denying to admitting that all was not well, it marked the beginning of a process of reappraisal. This though, was often accompanied by strong feelings of confusion and, at first, even resistance, as all the alternatives to their dysfunctional behavior appeared more frightening than the status quo. Gradually, however, a preferable alternative began to crystallize, and although the hurdles still seemed insurmountable, they had at least broken the stalemate.

Step 2: The Focal Event

Among the executives we have dealt with, accepting the need for change was generally not enough for them to take an active step toward changing their situation. They needed a push, and this often came in the form of what may be described as a "focal event." While the expression signals a significant conscious happening that triggers change, the reality is frequently less overt: often the focal event is only identified retrospectively as a milestone in their journey.

Here, the "last straw" may be a more appropriate metaphor, because it indicates that when a person is prepared—if not actually *ready*—to take a decisive step, the triggering event can be relatively minor. In fact, it is just the tipping point, the final push toward action. We have observed that, whereas major events can certainly be focal events, it is often more minor but cumulative occurrences that eventually make a person ripe for initiating change. These facilitating factors act as enablers for a person's long-delayed first step. Thus, while such an event is often seemingly minor, it frequently proves to be the catalyst in the change process.

> *Although a focal event is objectively perceived as minor, it is subjectively experienced as significant because it calls attention to a problem that has been simmering for a long time.*

Among our clients, this focal event commonly involved someone important to the person in question—an incident that, because it was perceived as a threat, led to a re-evaluation of the behavior that caused distress. One woman, for example, recognized the sudden death of her boss and mentor as her focal point; she saw in that death a judgment of her own over-dedication to the workplace. The crystallization of her discontent centered around this focal event, which magnified the existing problem and provided the impetus for change.

A person's focal event can also be seen as a kind of "screen memory"—an incident that is symbolic of the experienced problem. Although it is *objectively perceived* as minor, it is *subjectively experienced* as significant because it calls attention to a problem that has been simmering for a long time. It precipitates a moment of insight and leads to a reinterpretation of the person's life history. Of course, some focal events—such as the death of a co-worker, as in the above example, or personal illness—are objectively as well as subjectively significant. Others, however, may be unremarkable or even mundane. When discussed in a group session, their fellow participants can offer a supportive means of reinterpreting those events.

It is at this point in the process that the person in question becomes ready to act. He or she has acquired the inner strength to embark on change with conviction. Through the steps and focal points discussed above, the individual's resistance to change has been weakened. Whereas before there may only have been a sense of helplessness and hopelessness, new possibilities now emerge. Emotional energy can be transferred from those "concerns" of the past (such as dysfunctional behaviors) to aspects of the present and the future. Consequently, the person feels as if they have been freed from the heavy burden that was constantly weighing them down and is now mentally ready to tackle a more constructive future.

Step 3: The "Public" Declaration of Intent

Interviews with people who have undergone significant personal change suggest that a good indicator of their commitment to change is a *public* expression of their *intent* to change. The exact form and action required to enact change may not yet be clear, however the strength of their desire to do so marks this as a valuable step. Communicating openly to others what they plan to do indicates a strong degree of acceptance of the problem and signifies that the speaker is willing to defend his or her new way of looking at things. It indicates not only that the person has come to terms with his or her problems, but also that he or she is ready to take new initiatives.

> *A good indicator of a person's commitment to change is a public expression of their intent to change.*

Making a public commitment to a group stating their readiness to change is crucial because it doubles momentum and motivation. It is powerful not only because it makes explicit the willingness of the person to confront their situation but also because it enlists the support of others to reinforce those intentions. By formally making other people aware of a desire for change, there is a confirmation that their current situation is no longer valid or helpful, and that they need to adapt their attitude to new conditions. Furthermore, the pronouncement of their wish and intention to change publicly sets themselves an ultimatum: go through with it (whatever the change may be) or lose face. Take excessive drinking as an example. If a person states their wish and intent to give up an addiction to alcohol, acquaintances who approve of that decision are less likely to offer him or her a drink, and some may comment on it if they note the individual's resolve weakening. Another example would be if a person states to the group their wish and intent to be more assertive; the supporting members of the group are likely to remind that person of their tendency toward conflict-avoidant behavior should they see them failing to speak out. "Going public" with one's intentions, therefore, reinforces one's personal determination while enlisting a wider support network. We have seen this in our practice and encourage it as a valuable stage in the change process.

Step 4: The Inner Journey

These personal resolutions set the stage for a reappraisal of goals and envisioning of new alternatives. This inner journey is characterized by a crystallization of an individual's discontent, new insight into its causes, and increased self-knowledge.

Step 5: The Internalization of Change

The end result of working through these psychological processes may be summed up in *Step 5: an internalization of change*. The mindset of the person has changed, and a new way of looking at things has been adopted and internalized (see Fig. 9.1 for an overview of these individual stages of change).

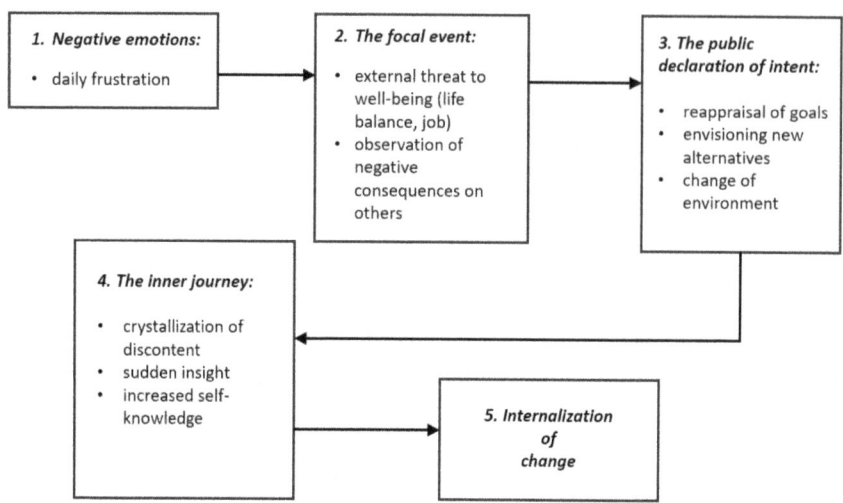

Fig. 9.1 Individual stages of change

The British Prime Minister, Winston Churchill, once said that "to improve is to change, so to be perfect is to have changed often."[1] Change is both a continuous process and an unavoidable fact of life. Although it can be painful at times, nothing is more frustrating than remaining stuck. What it is important to realize is that change brings opportunity. If we want to progress and develop in life, we need to step out of our comfort zone and understand change as intrinsic to living, or to quote Heraclitus, "all is flux, nothing stays still [πάντα χωρεῖ καὶ οὐδὲν μένει]."[2]

> *Change is both a continuous process and an unavoidable fact of life. Although it can be painful at times, nothing is more frustrating than remaining stuck.*

---

[1] Winston Churchill (June 23, 1925). His complete speeches, 1897–1963, edited by Robert Rhodes James, Chelsea House ed., vol. 4 (1922–1928), p. 3706. During a debate with Philip Snowden, 1st Viscount Snowden.

[2] Heraclitus as quoted by Plato in: Plato (1921/c. 388–367 BC). "Cratylus." In *Plato in Twelve Volumes*, Vol. 12. Trans. Harold N. Fowler. London, William Heinemann Ltd, §402a.

10

Creating a Transitional Space

All at once my position rose on me like a ghost. Anomalous, desolate, almost blank of hope, it stood. What was I doing here alone in great London? What should I do on the morrow? What prospects had I in life? What friends had I on earth? Whence did I come? Whither should I go? What should I do?

I wet the pillow, my arms, and my hair with rushing tears. A dark interval of bitter thought followed this burst; but I did not regret the step taken, nor wish to retract it. A strong, vague persuasion that it was better to go forward than backward, and that I could go forward—that a way, however narrow and difficult, would in time open—predominated over other feelings.
—Charlotte Brontë

The one self-knowledge worth having is to know one's own mind.
—Francis Herbert Bradley

Il faut bien que je supporte deux ou trois chenilles si je veux connaître les papillons. [Well, I must endure the presence of a few caterpillars if I wish to become acquainted with the butterflies.]
—Antoine de Saint-Exupéry

Nasruddin and the Finding of Joy

In a fabled Sufi story, there is a central character called Nasruddin, who, while eating at a restaurant in his town, met a man he had not seen before. They began talking about anything and everything, and soon the man began to confide in Nasruddin. He mentioned that he was a merchant from a nearby town, and, though he had grown very rich, he was sad and miserable.

He told Nasruddin that he had taken all his money and left to become a traveler in search of happiness but was still yet to find it.

Listening to the merchant, Nasruddin suddenly grabbed the man's bag containing all his money and belongings and ran off with it. The man was clearly startled, but then chased after him in alarm. Nasruddin had a head start though and was soon out of the man's sight. He hid behind some rocks and saw from afar where the merchant was going. Nasruddin knew the roads well, including the one the merchant was taking. He left the bag in the middle of the road for the man to find, then hid behind a tree.

When the man caught up to where Nasruddin had been, he found the bag, and his face turned instantly from distress to joy. As the man danced in celebration Nasruddin thought to himself, "Joy was right there all along for him to find."

Reframing and Encouragement

Nasruddin reframed the merchant's situation in this story. This is relevant to some of the techniques that can be used in coaching interventions to encourage people toward greater self-understanding.

First, we try to create an environment in which people feel relatively at ease talking about their feelings, anxieties, and concerns. If necessary, we use supportive techniques such as Nasruddin's demonstration of positive reframing, encouragement, anticipation, or rehearsal as a means of learning to deal with difficult situations.

Reframing is a cognitive technique employed to assist the person in diffusing or sidestepping painful situations. Encouragement includes reassurance, praise, and empathic comments that make people feel better about themselves and enhance self-esteem. However, a note of caution in regard to offering praise: it is important that, when given, it is meaningful, and pertains to something that the person considers worthy of praise. Typical empathic comments include: "That must have been very hard for you." "I guess you must have been quite scared." Or, "It sounds like you handled that situation well." Anticipation allows a person to move through new situations hypothetically, and role-play allows him or her to consider different ways of responding to a certain event. This kind of scenario building is a preparatory technique in that it gives people the chance to practice certain interactions with a view to reducing some of the anxiety. To envision worst and best scenarios can be quite enlightening. Rehearsal of this nature allows a person to consider the most appropriate ways of engaging in future events, as well as expanding his or her adaptive repertoire.

The Challenge of Transcendence

If an individual is to instate meaningful change, they need to recognize whether there are patterns of interaction with others that act to reinforce maladaptive attitudes and feelings toward themselves and others. The sooner these are identified, the greater the chances of altering these patterns. We strenuously maintain that therapeutic learning is experiential learning—the person changes as he or she works through emotionally painful experiences and ingrained interpersonal behavior. The challenge for the group is to promote more satisfying experiences, yet the interaction with the group may give rise to unexpected, anticipated, feared, and sometimes hoped for outcomes.

> *Therapeutic learning is experiential learning—the person changes as he or she works through emotionally painful experiences and ingrained interpersonal behavior.*

Actively Working on the Problem

Far reaching personality changes can be achieved through the active pursuit of a chosen theme in a coaching/therapy session. In the process, systematic challenge to the person's defenses occurs and extreme attention is given to the presence of transferential reactions. While confrontation and clarification are directed toward the conscious material brought up by the person, the interpretation is aimed at clarifying hidden connections. From a clinical perspective, a successful interpretation will intertwine the cognitive and emotional dimensions of the problem.

Timing is also critical for successful interventions. Executive coaches need to realize that interpretations will not be heard, let alone be effective, when the individual is in the middle of an emotional crisis. When there is too much emotion, integration of the interpretation will be difficult. Thus, it is important "to strike when the iron is cold."

> *Executive coaches need to realize that interpretations will not be heard, let alone be effective, when the individual is in the middle of an emotional crisis.*

What is critical to the process is that the person in the "hot seat" perceives that both the members of the group and the facilitator have his or her best interests at heart and see it as a safe place for emotion and experiment. When the dynamics of the group become too confrontational, some people may become too anxious to be able to "play" and to learn effectively. When participants gain confidence in the benefits of examining dysfunctional behavior patterns collaboratively, they will be more open to confronting the emotions and fantasies associated with these patterns. The result is progressively more potential to modify conflict-ridden attitudes and behavior, and to develop responses that are more adaptive and flexible to changing circumstances. Confidence is critical to experimenting with new ways of doing things.

> *Confidence is critical to experimenting with new ways of doing things.*

The Group as Projective Screen

Although coaches are there in a group session to provide interpretations, the insights of one's peers are also important. In the group setting, executives often have less resistance to learning about themselves from peers than they do from people in a position of authority. Consequently, one of the challenges for facilitators is to resist making an interpretation and to wait instead for the members of the group to arrive at solutions. As the saying goes, wisdom consists of two parts: having a great deal to say, and not saying it!

> *Executives often have less resistance to learning about themselves from peers than they do from people in a position of authority.*

Confidence that a group is a safe space to experiment, however, is something that needs to be built up. In our practice we try to create a safe transitional space that will foster these dynamics and allow participants to feel at ease.

In the knowledge that everybody will be somewhat anxious at the start of a session, we try to create a sense of play. For example, tasking participants with a fun icebreaking activity, such as drawing a personal portrait, may encourage individual creativity. Then, thinking about the various facets important to their life sets the stage for the next phase, which focuses on the sharing of some of the 360-degree feedback results. If this process is done well, the group becomes a "holding environment"—a transitional space provided to contain the emotional experiences of each participant.

> As the saying goes, wisdom consists of two parts: having a great deal to say, and not saying it!

Once a great deal of trust has been established among the members of the group, we can begin to describe this as a "transitional space." This idea is derived from the illusionary transitional world of childhood; the play area between reality and fantasy created by parents and children. This transitional space is a means of resolving the developmental challenges of childhood while acting as an incubator of creative thought. It is the place where processes such as symbolization, make-believe, illusion, daydreaming, playfulness, curiosity, imagination, and wonder all start. The challenge in these interventions is to recreate this illusionary space and encourage participants to express themselves in ways that are out of the ordinary.

The transitional space provides great opportunities for helping participants come out of their comfort zones and experiment with new ways of doing things. They will be encouraged to examine their own behavior and to develop more varied and flexible defensive systems for dealing with the vicissitudes of life. In particular, it will facilitate greater self-understanding: the person who is the center of attention will have the opportunity to re-experience problematic relationship dilemmas in the context of the group, thereby gaining the fresh insights that might lead to greater freedom of action in life.

Listening with the Third Ear

Every participant who presents an issue in this transitional space, or sphere of illusion, has some effect on the other group members. This is largely by way of the subtle, semi-conscious reactions known as "countertransference reactions." Thereafter, these countertransference activities go on to shape the observations of each member. The emotional responses elicited by any given presentation reveal the various sensitivities of the other members; they also offer evidence of the presenter's attempts (both conscious and unconscious) to evoke certain reactions in others.

One of the most fundamental ways in which we learn is by observation followed by imitation. Here, the previously mentioned mirror neurons come into play (see Chapter 6). These are a particular type of brain cell that responds equally whether we personally perform an action or if we witness someone else perform the same action. Thus, our mirror neurons literally "mirror" the behavior of the other's, as though the observer itself were acting. As such, they are thought to play a significant role in learning and intention understanding, speech and language evolution, and emotional intelligence and empathy.

> *One of the most fundamental ways in which we learn is by observation followed by imitation.*

It is with these mirror neurons that we engage in primitive forms of communication. Whether it is labeled as "countertransference" or "projective identification," the process implies that aspects of what a person experiences are "expelled" and "deposited" in other people. Thus, the initiator of communication causes the receivers to narratively transport feelings that are similar to his or her own. This has the potential to create a state of reverie in which participants allow themselves to be led by personal memories and imagination. "Using themselves as instruments" in this way encourages them to build empathy and compassion, enabling the recipients to "read" what the initiator is communicating. Because intuitive thoughts and ideas are based on the primitive processes of mirror neurons, participants are encouraged to "listen with the third ear"; that is, to understand at an intuitive level the presenter's psychic reality.

The conjunction of countertransference reactions, including feelings of compassion and empathy—instigated by these mirror neurons—allows the other members of the group to imagine themselves in the presenter's place, experiencing the same thoughts and desires. Particularly sensitive participants can penetrate—by thought and feeling—the inner life of the presenter, while retaining enough objectivity to create hypotheses and theories about that inner life. The information provided as group members talk about their feelings and fantasies in response to a presentation helps the presenter better understand what his or her key issues are. In fact, these emotional responses represent one of the most important tools in a participant's efforts to change.

The spectrum of these countertransference reactions ranges from subtle responses such as vague feelings of anxiety, sleepiness, boredom, disgust, sadness, futility, helplessness, or disdain, to more powerful responses such as becoming angry, feeling intimidated, experiencing sexual arousal, or not listening. More dramatic responses still may include direct conflict with a fellow member, leaving the room in a huff, or a paralyzing fear of losing control and causing harm. Yet, over time, participants become increasingly proficient at translating these subtle (and not so subtle) signals into imagery that has meaning, and they learn to interpret not only what is expressed verbally and non-verbally, but also what is avoided.

> *By using the group as a projective screen, an extremely complex interpersonal encounter takes place that intertwines past and present experiences.*

If we return to the case of the female CEO mentioned in Chapter 8, every time her tendency toward irrational anger came to the fore, she was reminded by the members of the group of it happening. These reminders in the main session, in the small groups, and during social occasions thereafter provided more self-understanding, and the opportunity to practice more constructive behavior and work through chronic personality problems. With increased understanding of individual behavioral patterns, the relationship between the facilitators and other members of the group would illicit an ever more profound learning process. In contrast to one-to-one situations, the group setting provides a breadth of experiences and interpretations relevant to the here-and-now. It gives individuals the opportunity to work through many different manifestations of their problem and, in this way, connects insights gained within the group with real-world experiences and historical data.

By using the group as a projective screen, an extremely complex interpersonal encounter takes place that intertwines past and present experiences. As people try to unravel past life situations, current life situations, and transferential patterns, they attempt to make conscious their hidden feelings and wishes, defensive reactions, and the underlying causes of anxiety. In the process, participants have to psychologically integrate their feelings as to what was, what is, and what will be.

Inevitably, memories are closely tied to knowledge and integral to our understanding of what was. They often consist of events of importance to us and significant people in our lives and the emotions attached to these. As we review and unravel the threads of our past, present, and future, we are also expanding our awareness of what was, what is, and what will be. By facing up to the past we will acquire some mastery of the present and be freer to shape the future.

Change requires conscious and unconscious conceptual processing, and, if we are to recognize new realities and practice new ways of thinking and acting, demands many repetitions. Experimenting with new behaviors needs to be tried and assessed in what will necessarily be a period of psychological growth and increased creativity. This can take some time as the flow of pathological behavior patterns may disappear, reappear in another form, only to disappear again until the most constructive is identified.

> *As we review and unravel the threads of our past, present, and future, we are also expanding our awareness of what was, what is, and what will be. By facing up to the past we will acquire some mastery of the present and be freer to shape the future.*

Consolidating the Change

The critical task that follows this point involves maintaining the acquired gains. The endeavor for each of the participants is to modify their inner script, but this transformation can only take place once a new way of looking at things has been internalized. Internalization is a gradual process by which external interactions between the person and others are absorbed and then replaced by internal representations of these interactions. This new way of looking at things has become part of one's internal psychic structure. The retelling of one's own story and listening to the stories of others and recognizing similarities contributes to this process of internalization.

After this process of internalization has taken place, do people feel changed? It is hard to tell. When I talk to people at follow-up sessions, they may say: "I'm basically the same," but then add "I do feel somewhat stronger about what I can and can't do. I have more confidence in my abilities. Previously, in the office, I always felt somewhat like an impostor that was merely acting in a role." They might note how this has changed, reflecting "that it is quite different now. I enjoy what I am doing. I guess something must have happened. My wife tells me so. I play much more with my children. I have a more positive outlook on life, am no longer so opinionated, and find it easier to open up to others. But have I changed? I really don't know."

The challenge for each individual is to hold on to the acquired insights when the group is no longer there to keep them on target. Most people are able to hold on to the gains they have made, although we anticipate some erosion over time. Interestingly, with the greater clarity they have acquired about the issues they need to deal with, a significant number of participants make the decision to see a coach, counselor, or therapist on a regular basis to keep them on course. Furthermore, many appear to enjoy having sparring partners who are not tiptoeing around them.

> *Feeling better about ourselves allows for a broader perspective on our relationships with others and facilitates different and better ways of responding.*

What Does a Positive Outcome Entail?

What can be considered a positive outcome is a better quality of life. This might mean increased self-esteem, a reduction in anxiety, fewer symptoms of stress, and an increase in adaptive functioning. It is also indicated by the person's ability to play. The automatic defense mechanisms which had been a means of coping (albeit ineffectively) with life, will have been replaced by a new awareness of choice. Feeling better about ourselves allows for a broader perspective on our relationships with others and facilitates different and better ways of responding. Fundamentally, it is about better relationships with family, friends, and people at work. The poet Martial succinctly stated that, "Tomorrow's life is too late. Live today [Sera nimis vita est crastina: vive hodie]."[1] Happiness and success in life are not the result of what we have, but rather of how we live.

> *Happiness and success in life are not the result of what we have, but rather of how we live.*

---

[1] Martial (1897/c. 80–140 AD). *The Epigrams of Martial Translated into English Prose*. London: George Bell and Sons, Book I, 15.

11

Navigating the Maze of Organizational Transformation

Come, come, my conservative friend, wipe the dew off your spectacles, and see that the world is moving.
—Elizabeth Cady Stanton

If the thought of sorrow is waylaying (spoiling) joy, (yet) it is making preparations for joy.
It violently sweeps thy house clear of (all) else, in order that new joy from the source of good may enter in.
It scatters the yellow leaves from the bough of the heart, in order that incessant green leaves may grow.
It uproots the old joy, in order that new delight may march in from the Beyond.
—Rúmí

Either do not attempt at all, or go through with it.
[Aut non tentaris, aut perfice.]
—Ovid

The Beetle and the Pupa

The beetle asked the pupa, who was hanging on the stem of a plant, "why don't you move? Why are you just hanging on this plant?" The pupa responded that she was waiting for the perfect moment to split her chrysalis, unfold her wings, and to take flight as a butterfly. It took some time for the beetle to process this information. While he was reflecting on what the pupa had said, she added that she wasn't just fluttering around. No, on the contrary, she said, she would do much more. "Not only will I flutter from flower to flower to get at the nectar that will fuel my flight, but by doing so, I will have a much wider impact."

When the beetle asked what she meant by having a much bigger impact, she said: "In this world of ours, everything is interrelated. While it might look as if my actions are purely selfish, in reality, what I am doing ensures that many flowers will bloom in the future, that fruits grow on the trees, and that, in the larger scheme of things, my activities bring new plants into existence." The pupa added, "when the time has come to spread my wings, I will make a small contribution toward transforming the world as it is known presently."

Her commentary silenced the beetle. He had come to realize that what seemed like a minor activity had, in reality, wide-reaching impact; micro could, by increments, become macro.

This analogy can be used to draw a parallel between the way individuals change and the way change takes place in organizations. Similar to individual transformation, organizational change tends to be sequential in nature. Equally similar is that the change process is often initiated by a sense of discomfort in the organizational system, and the resulting stress acts as a lever setting wider change in motion.

However, pushing that lever is easier said than done because, as with individual change, there are many potential resistances to deal with. At first glance, for example, the organizational participants may not recognize that a transformation will be in their best interest, and even those who are aware that an organization could function better, can find infinite ways of avoiding the issue. There may also be fear that the proclaimed benefits of a particular change will not outweigh its costs.

> *Organizational participants may not recognize that a transformation will be in their best interest, and even those who are aware that an organization could function better, can find infinite ways of avoiding the issue.*

The Organizational Change Journey

As has been mentioned previously, change is unfamiliar and raises any number of insecurities, manifesting in a lot of resistance. In order to break this impasse, it must be made clear to all those involved that the present state of affairs is creating more problems than diving into the unknown. The people working in the organization need to realize the implications of inaction and recognize that not acting is also a form of action. In short, they have to be made aware of the costs of not changing.

> *It must be made clear to all those involved that the present state of affairs is creating more problems than diving into the unknown.*

Creating Dissatisfaction

We have all heard the saying, "no gain without pain." In the context of personal change this phrase has considerable truth. The willingness to change usually indicates a high level of stress—sufficient to motivate an individual to act. Just as discomfort with the status quo is the engine that drives individual change efforts, studying organizations that are prepared to undergo change suggests that stress acts in much the same way to drive organizational change. In spite of the ongoing "pain," however, many necessary organizational change processes are stalled because of defensive routines.

If such routines continue within an organization despite extreme discomfort, we can assume that the resistance stems from the key powerholders. They may be entrenched in behavior patterns that have previously proven effective but fail to realize that circumstances have changed and adaptation is needed. What might previously have been a recipe for successful performance has now become a disaster, and once good practices—for example, those in alignment with the economic environment—are no longer viable. (As someone once said in an adaptation of the Irish poet Oscar Wilde's words: "In this world there are only two tragedies. One is not getting what one wants, and the other is getting it.")[1] Yet, changing the mindset of an organization's powerholders will never be easy, and generally requires a strong jolt of some kind. Those favoring change must pressure the sceptics into seeing that the present state

---
[1] Oscar Wilde (1917/1892). *Lady Windermere's Fan.* London: Methuen & Co.

is no longer viable and that the alignment of organization and environment is off-center.

Awareness of the need for change is achieved most effectively by creating pressures both from within and from outside of the organization. Some of the external factors that can cause stress in organizations are threats from competitors, declining profits, decreasing market share, scarcity of resources, deregulation, the impact of technology, and problems with suppliers and consumer groups. Examples of internal pressures are ineffective leadership, morale problems, a high turnover of capable people, absenteeism, labor problems (such as strikes), increased political behavior in the company, and turf fights. These are all factors which inevitably negatively affect the mindset of the people in the organization. The resulting malaise corrodes the corporate culture and has an impact on patterns of decision-making. As these stressors cause increasing daily frustration, they reach a point when they can no longer be ignored. Gradually, many dissatisfied people within the organization realize that something needs to be done if they are to avert the risks currently endangering the future of the organization. This state of mind is the organizational equivalent of the individual's crystallization of discontent. Creating a shared mindset, characterized by collective ambition, commitment, and motivation, generates the sense of urgency that means action is necessary. At this stage of transformation, an external focus becomes critical.

> *Creating hope is essential if we are to break vicious cycles endemic across an organization.*

Engendering Hope

In this phase of the change process, creating hope is vital, and forming a new vision and mission is one way of doing this. Often this can be formulated with the help of external advisors. We have found creating hope to be essential if we are to break vicious cycles endemic across an organization. Key players in the organization—ideally those who hold positions of power, for example, the CEO—should be prepared to take on the role of change agents. Although people at other levels of the organization can (and sometimes must) take the initiative, the reality of power dynamics is such that members of the dominant coalition (particularly the CEO) are most effective at setting the change process in motion. After all, the extent of a person's authority, resource control, and the way his or her dependency relationships are constructed within the organization are all factors that heavily influence his or her power to effect change.

As change agents we help key powerholders ascertain the major challenges their organization is facing. We indicate points of stress that could be managed differently, and set out a clear picture of the negative consequences should they fail to act. One method is that of benchmarking against other organizations as a means of illustrating the inefficiencies of their present state. Actively showing employees of an organization the successful initiatives of their competitors is crucial to them understanding the potential to create a more advanced and efficient organization; at this stage, our role is to clarify all that is difficult about their existing state.

Change agents must tread carefully, however, if they are to establish change at a level that is tolerable to all parties. Regardless of their discomfort in their current position, those who feel overwhelmed by anxiety may simply tune the problems out, and with them the learning potential that can be facilitated by executive coaching.

> *By referring to the organization's past accomplishments while presenting a new way of doing things, leaders can create a sense of hope; a dual approach which makes for a sense of new beginning.*

As a means of mitigating against excessive stress, the people who drive the change effort must thus present a viable alternative to the existing situation. The creation of hope will be essential. A collective ambition needs to be created, with a view to drawing up a collaborative plan. At this point it is crucial that the people who work in the organization perceive the change program as something realistic and not simply a "pie in the sky" proposition.

When developing the outlines of a change process, we also suggest that the change leaders need to reframe not just the positive aspects of the change effort but also the cultural guidelines that people in the organization have become used to. They need to create pride in the organization's history, yet also point out how holding onto tradition can anchor the organization in the past. By referring to the organization's past accomplishments while presenting a new way of doing things, leaders can create a sense of hope; a dual approach which makes for a sense of new beginning.

One important factor to be addressed by executives is their fear regarding their future career prospects. Both the organization and the consultants must appease these as common and inevitable concerns. Reinforcing the personal implications of resisting change is a means of preventing the all-too-common ostrich policy, whereby individuals actively avoid acknowledging the need for change. Leaders must talk instead about what effect ignoring external threats is likely to have on their future career in the organization. At the same time, they should emphasize the opportunities that will be opened up by acting to counteract those threats. A new psychological contract, implying mutual obligations and commitments (explicit and implicit) between the employees and the organization, must be established. Also, the new values required to make the transformation effort a success have to be clearly spelled out in order to win support of the change process.

Repetition of these messages will also be important. People should be regularly assessed as to how they are dealing with the consequences of loss that change implies—every visual and verbal opportunity to emphasize this message must be taken.

> *People should be regularly assessed as to how they are dealing with the consequences of loss that change implies—every visual and verbal opportunity to emphasize this message must be taken.*

In order to provide a focus, we suggest that issues are addressed in an understandable way. Leaders must create symbols that represent the new organization yet also accentuate elements of continuity between the old and the new. In other words, getting people on board may demand a certain amount of "theater," or symbolic action, which serves both as a means of clarifying goals and of drawing people into the process.

One illustration of this in action involves the CEO of a consumer products company who began making regular store visits during which he talked frequently with potential customers. This interaction was his way of emphasizing that the new or more central value of customer focus was not just another empty slogan. His emphasis on customer satisfaction quickly caught on, reverberating throughout the company.

In another scenario, a CEO who was driving a corporate transformation effort asked all his executives to write a letter of resignation to the "old" company and a letter of application for the "new" one. This activity led them to rethink what was wrong with the company and encouraged them to reflect on how it might be turned into a high-performance organization and had a powerful impact. Additionally, calling on employees to "rally round" and give their input should not be underestimated as a means of motivating and involving them.

In communicating their message, leaders must focus on clear, compelling reasons for change, and allay fears that tradition is being abandoned for no good reason. To dispel such fears, the executives driving the change effort should try to build on aspects of the existing culture that can be carried across to the new organizational vision. Employees must perceive the entire change process as one informed by solid corporate values. They must see that the aim is not only to build and maintain a competitive advantage but also to address the individual needs of the people who will be affected. Finally, they must come to realize that there are boundaries to the change process, and that the proposed change effort has clearly defined parameters.

> *Being committed to honest, focused, and persuasive communication pays dividends to those spearheading a change effort. In reality, most people will have at least a basic awareness of the major problems facing the organization and, despite their lingering resistance, will then be more prepared to accept the need for change.*

Being committed to honest, focused, and persuasive communication pays dividends to those spearheading a change effort. In reality, most people will have at least a basic awareness of the major problems facing the organization and, despite their lingering resistance, will then be more prepared to accept the need for change.

Carrying out the Transformation

After leaders have convinced their people of the need for change, we can work toward the next step—aligning the crucial players behind their new view of the future. They must put the appropriate structure in place to help the organization's participants actuate the new vision. Leaders must build coalitions with other key powerholders in the organization who can then help to disseminate commitment and cooperation throughout the organization.

To expedite the process, leaders driving a change effort need to empower their subordinates by sharing information, minimizing secrecy, and delegating responsibility. They should keep surprises to a minimum, clearly delineate expectations, and maintain a dialogue that is both ongoing and genuinely (rather than superficially) two-way. Furthermore, they need to communicate the salient values by setting an example of clarity and consistency. In other words, those who drive the process have to "walk the talk."

Employee participation and involvement are the key success factors to organizational commitment. People at all levels of the organization—not only those at the top—should be involved in the change effort, tackling first a joint diagnosis of the problem. Participation is likely to be more appealing if the reward structure is aligned with the desired future organization: for example, leaders can offer various incentives (financial or career wise) to employees who support the change effort, thereby signaling the benefits of change. Building the right competencies, practices, and attitudes becomes crucial at this stage. Those who are willing to acquire these new competencies should be rewarded just as those who have other required skills; they will then serve as models to others.

> *By stretching people's potential and offering them an opportunity to be more ambitious, leaders encourage their workforce to rise to the challenge of change.*

It has been observed that small wins have a ripple effect within an organization. Hence, leaders are advised to divide a major change effort into bite-size portions, thereby making the overall task more palatable. Visible improvements—again, small wins—help convince people of the feasibility of the change effort. While this "small wins" process is in motion however, the people in charge should also meet consistently high-performance expectations. By stretching people's potential and offering them an opportunity to be more ambitious, leaders encourage their workforce to rise to the challenge. This simultaneous approach benefits both the organization and the individual: reaching one's goals engenders considerable personal satisfaction; seeing how they fit within a longer change trajectory reinforces and motivates further progress (see Fig. 11.1 for an overview of the corporate change process).

Staging Transformative Events

We have learned from experience that if the people in charge of the change effort apply the techniques discussed above, most of the organizational participants will have probably evolved from contemplation of change to action. They are committed to, and working on, overcoming existing problems, changing personal behavior, and making changes in the organization's structure, strategy, and culture. If the leaders of the organization feel the need to expedite the change process, however, with our clinical approach we often

The Corporate Transformation Process

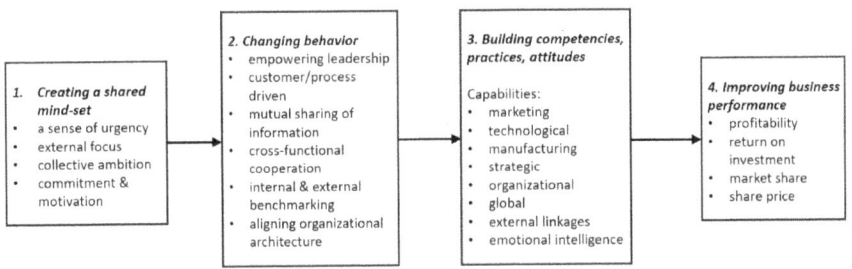

Fig. 11.1 The corporate transformation process

try to "imitate life" by "staging" a **transformative event**. This can be done in various ways: it can be an off-site gathering at which members of senior management announce plans for a new organization, or it can take the form of a series of workshops, a seminar, or a meeting run by our associates. Whatever the format, such a staged, transformative event should allow for—indeed, mandate and focus on—strategic dialogue between top management (particularly the CEO and members of the executive committee) and their subordinates.

As a forum for feedback and critique, strategic dialogue offers the opportunity for a more focused organization-wide involvement. The resistance that people feel not only to initiating change themselves but to *being* changed is lessened by such involvement, because it gives participants a sense of control over their destiny. Since strategic dialogue is based on a direct feedback loop with senior management, it permits open and informed discussion of the challenges facing the company. Topics perceived as non-discussable in the day-to-day work context can be put forward and addressed, thus diminishing the level of employee anxiety (especially among those who have the will to change but who are afraid that they lack the necessary competence). Furthermore, strategic dialogue offers an opportunity to mourn the old way of doing things, allowing nostalgia for the past to be voiced while actively cultivating a sense of excitement about future challenges to come. Enthusiasm within any group is a valuable form of glue and instates a common goal.

> *Strategic dialogue offers an opportunity to mourn the old way of doing things, allowing nostalgia for the past to be voiced whist actively cultivating a sense of excitement about future challenges to come.*

A transformative event provides the opportunity to address more systematically a number of issues that have already been raised. First, even if most people seem to have bought in to the notion that the organization's present state is unsatisfactory and unsustainable, during the strategic dialogue, leaders should re-emphasize this crucial point. Second, it is an opportunity to reiterate the need for company-wide commitment to a redefined corporate vision, mission, and new cultural values. Third, leaders should work with focal-event participants to determine whether the appropriate organizational design, systems, and workforce are in place. Fourth, they should address the question, given the need for change, of whether the company possesses the right mix of competencies. If not, is the training and development program that helps employees acquire the necessary competencies (and thus reinforces their belief in their own skills to change) adequate, or do outsiders with specialized expertise need to be brought into the organization? Fifth, attention should be paid to the question of whether performance appraisal and reward systems need to be modified to encourage alignment of behavior with the new circumstances. Finally, are resources, including leadership, available to support the kind of change that is required? (See Fig. 11.2 for a summary of such an assessment process.)

> *A public declaration of what people hope to achieve and contribute to the transformation process strengthens commitment to the organizational change effort; it reinforces the intent to change simply by making it highly visible.*

As has been explained in the previous chapters, encouraging individuals to make a public declaration of their intent to change during these events will also have a powerful effect in the context of these dialogues. As in the case of personal change efforts, a public declaration of what people hope to achieve and contribute to the transformation process strengthens commitment to the organizational change effort; it reinforces the intent to change simply by making it highly visible. A public declaration of intent alone is not good enough, however. It has to be supported, include a means of measuring progress, and ideally involve a detailed personal action plan as to how each declaration will be achieved. After all, what is not measured rarely gets done.

The Assessment Process

Criteria	Question: To what extent …
Barriers to change	…do people in the organization recognize the need to change?
Triggers of change	…are inside and outside forces pressuring the organization?
Degree of dissatisfaction	…is the organization as a whole dissatisfied with the present status quo?
Common vision, culture, and mission	…does the organization have shared values, goals, and expectations?
Structure and process	…does the organization have the correct organizational design and process in place?
Competencies	…does the organization have the right mix of competencies: skills, attitudes, and knowledge?
Aligning behavior	…do performance appraisal and reward systems encourage the right behavior?
Capacity for change	…does the organization have the ability and resources to handle the kind of change that is required?
Leadership	…does the organization have the right quantity and quality of leadership?

Fig. 11.2 The assessment process

An important point in regard to managing a staged transformative event is that blaming others for existing difficulties is unproductive. It is easy for individuals to be drawn into the deep-seated notion that "the enemy is us," when energy would be better spent working collaboratively toward the new corporate vision.

> *What is not measured rarely gets done.*

Our sessions concerning organizations hoping to undergo major change initiatives offer the opportunity to explore the extent to which problems can be traced back to what were originally good practices but are now out of alignment. Strategic dialogue should not be overwhelmingly negative, however: focal-event workshops should facilitate a process of self-discovery of both the good and the bad. People must be allowed the time and opportunity to reflect on what made the organization great, while acknowledging that what was effective in the past socio-economic climate may no longer be appropriate to the present circumstances. The opportunity to reminisce, learn from, and mourn the past allows people to build on the old and commit to creating the new. To this end, strategic dialogue should permit freedom of expression, where participants feel able to talk about their fears, nostalgia, and grief for the past, but also share and encourage excitement for the future. However, this will not be a rapid process—it takes considerable time for a new conception of the organization to be fully metabolized, and to go from superficial adoption of a new state of affairs to deep internalization.

> *The opportunity to reminisce, learn from, and mourn the past allows people to build on the old and commit to creating the new.*

Given the potential impact a staged transformation process may have, company executives need first to address the delicate question of leadership roles. This is particularly sensitive if there is a lack of confidence in the current CEO to drive the change effort. In fact, if we consider organizations that have successfully executed dramatic change, it is often the case that an outsider has been brought in for exactly that purpose. The main benefit is that outsiders are far less (if at all) bound to a particular way of doing things in an organization; they have less sentimental attachment, less interpersonal loyalty, and are prepared to push the requisite levers to set change in motion.

Transforming the Past

The corporate world of today is one of constant change; in a climate of discontinuities and shifting politics, organizations have to adapt their behavior in order to maintain a competitive advantage. An organization that is firmly stuck in the behavior patterns of the past is doomed to failure. The greatest challenge organizational leaders face can thus be seen as something of a paradox wherein previous success leads to complacency and arrogance but then becomes a threat to the future success of the organization. Given the ease with which these circumstances evolve, a secure grasp of the dynamics of change is a necessity for any leader, and executives who have a poor understanding of change processes will be at a competitive disadvantage.

> *In a climate of discontinuities and shifting politics, organizations have to adapt their behavior in order to maintain a competitive advantage. An organization that is firmly stuck in the behavior patterns of the past is doomed to failure.*

Creating the kind of organization that incorporates change into its core values is one of the greatest challenges faced by today's leaders. Yet, when oriented toward change, an organization's culture becomes regenerative. Instead of enacting the turmoil and anxiety of full-blown transformation processes, we believe that organizations need continuous, gradual change. When in harmony, this is a culture which occurs naturally—both leaders and followers learn to ask themselves habitually whether their way of doing things is efficient, effective, and firmly embedded in reality. Organizations that remain wholly aligned with their values, vision, and context minimize the problem of environmental "creep," meaning incremental changes in conditions which end up creating a major catastrophe or crisis.

The ultimate challenge, therefore, is to create an organizational mindset in which people's creative capabilities are identified and fully deployed, and where change is welcomed and desired. This, as we have seen, is not an easy proposition. To prevent rigidification and routinization—or, in short, prevent employees from settling down too firmly at their desks—leaders need to cultivate a culture where people are encouraged to challenge established ways of doing things.

Organizations that foster an atmosphere of constructive conflict—in which people do not take the recommendations of their powerholders for granted, where they question what their leaders have to say, and where strategic dialogue is the rule rather than the exception—will be in the best position to remain aligned with the corporate environment, however much or often it changes. Organizations characterized by this sort of constructive dialogue will unearth missed opportunities and inform top executives of the concerns of the employees. When such a mindset prevails, it serves as an early warning system of the need for change. This constant testing of the status quo makes organizational preventive maintenance possible and creates an atmosphere of continuous learning.

> *Organizations that foster an atmosphere of constructive conflict—in which people do not take the recommendations of their powerholders for granted, where they question what their leaders have to say, and where strategic dialogue is the rule rather than the exception—will be in the best position to remain aligned with the corporate environment, however much or often it changes.*

Making such an organizational culture a viable proposition takes sustained effort, since change runs counter to the built-in conservatism of human behavior. Even while old resistances are breaking down, new ones are emerging. The danger of rigidification is ever present. As the Canadian-American economist John Kenneth Galbraith once remarked: "Faced with the choice between changing one's mind and proving that there is no need to do so, almost everyone gets busy on the proof."[2] People who understand the dynamics of change but who do not spend their time looking for proof, and who realize that the tremendous opportunities inherent in a proactive stance far outweigh the temporary sense of discomfort that accompanies it, will be the winners in this world of discontinuities.

If change is to be a positive force in organizations, it must be guided by imaginative, empathetic, and adaptive leadership. To grasp the opportunities and lessen the anxieties that come with change processes, leaders must have collaborative, problem solving, and influencing skills; an astute understanding of how to analyze complex processes and grasp the intricacies of the company's value chain; and the ability to deal with inefficiencies. They cannot do this alone: they must recognize interdependencies with other stakeholders in the organization and build organizations that motivate and empower employees to perform at peak capacity. Although we may be intrigued by people with charisma, in reality, most successful organizations are not those led by one, powerful, charismatic leader, but are the product of distributive, collective, and complementary leadership. The most effective organizations

---

[2] John Kenneth Galbraith (1971). *Economics, Peace and Laughter*. London: André Deutsch.

are team-oriented, whereby individuals' natural leadership styles and strengths are matched to particular roles and challenges, supported by a coaching culture within the organization. As rapid decision-making provides a considerable competitive advantage, effective teamwork will be essential to make these complex structures work. Moreover, what makes working in teams all the more challenging is that these teams have become increasingly diverse (i.e., culture, gender, age, education, and functional background) and more virtual. To deal with the complexity of these networking structures, the ability to create a constructive team environment will be critical for its success. However, the major challenge in creating well-functioning teams within these global, diverse, matrix-like structures is the emergence of paranoid thinking, the presence of silos, turf fights, and "constipated," slow decision-making processes. At all costs, these behavior patterns need to be avoided.

> *Most successful organizations are not those led by one, powerful, charismatic leader, but are the product of distributive, collective, and complementary leadership.*

The kind of cultural transformation needed to create high-performance organizations is not easy to accomplish because it necessitates changes at both micro and macro levels. Creating and sustaining a more inclusive corporate culture requires a high degree of openness, trust, and adaptability on the part of *all* the people in an organization. Here, executive group coaching can be a catalyst in the creation of a new cultural environment. It will have an extremely powerful impact in creating better leaders and more effective organizations.

Transformation will always be a difficult process, and as with most things in life, there will be many ups and downs. We know that the people who are experiencing these major change processes may feel frightened, dejected, and discouraged. Like any journey of discovery, there will be moments when we believe that we have climbed the greatest mountains, but also other moments when we seem to have fallen off the cliffs of despair. Still, what needs to be kept in mind is that transformation is the law of life.

> *There will be moments when we believe that we have climbed the greatest mountains, but also other moments when we seem to have fallen off the cliffs of despair. Still, what needs to be kept in mind is that transformation is the law of life.*

12

The Process of Letting Go

Nothing can bring you peace but yourself.
—Ralph Waldo Emerson

L'objet de la psychologie est de nous donner une idée toute autre des choses que nous connaissons le mieux.
[The purpose of psychology is to give us a completely different idea of the things we know best.]
—Paul Valéry

Let me tell you the secret of such so-called successes as there have been in my life, and here I believe I give you really good advice. It was to burn my boats and demolish my bridges behind me. Then one loses no time in looking behind, when one should have quite enough to do in looking ahead.
—Fridtof Nansen

The Two Travelers and the Stream

There is a well-known Zen story of two traveling monks who reached a bend in a stream that they needed to cross. At the crossing point stood a young woman who seemed unsure of how to proceed. The younger monk noticed the woman, said nothing, and walked by. The older monk, however, talked to her, then picked her up and put her on his back. He transported the young woman across the stream, to put her down on the other side. She thanked the older monk and went on her way.

As the two monks continued on their journey, the young monk was brooding and preoccupied. After several hours, unable to hold his silence, he spoke out.

"How could you put that attractive woman on your back?"

The older monk said, "I set the woman down hours ago. I let go. But why are you still carrying her?"

Letting Go

People need to decide to take control of the things they have the power to control instead of holding onto the things over which they don't have any control. Of course, to hold on, or "hang in," can be a sign of great strength. However, there will be times when it takes more strength to know when to let go. It is important to recognize that yesterday has passed; that today will be a new beginning. In fact, life's most important lessons are often about knowing when to hang on and when to let go.

> *There will be times when it takes more strength to know when to let go. It is important to recognize that yesterday has passed; that today will be a new beginning.*

Letting go of the old ways of doing things is not a simple cognitive process; it is, first and foremost, a sequential emotional process. As we have pointed out, organizational transformation, like personal change, often starts with a state of turmoil. With the anxiety levels rising, sometimes to the point of panic (for example, among those who fear for their jobs), normal organizational processes generally come to a halt or become ritualistic. People fall back into familiar routines, going through the motions they know well as a means of processing and dealing with news of impending change to come. At this early stage in the game, few people are ready to accept that a new way of doing things has become unavoidable.

When dramatic, transformative change happens, the most primitive and well-known response to shock (remember Wilfred Bion's description of the various modes that occur in groups—Chapter 4) is the "fight or flight" mode—a regressive tendency that can be applied to most unpredictable contexts, including organizational change. The other relevant behavioral reaction is that of the dependency mode. With leadership in mind, those in the dependency mode may wish for (and imagine that they have) an omnipotent leader who will set things right. Other features of dependency may be passivity and a lack of initiative or action.

Fight behavior, on the other hand, may be symptomized by a displacement of anger—that is, by blaming or scapegoating others for what is happening. People regressing to fight behavior often exhibit a great deal of irritability and bitterness. However, these emotions are often directed not toward the corporation itself (and the people and practices within it) but toward "others" who might be to blame. Customers, suppliers, the government, and competitors are all potential victims of the "fight" response. People resorting to fight behavior are not yet ready to accept their role in the situation. Instead, they waste their energy on internal politics and turf fights rather than addressing their real problems. Other people regress not to dependency or anger but to flight behavior—some may leave their organization at the first signs of stress, whereas others simply withdraw, participating little in office activities and redirecting their focus toward other things outside of work.

These modes of behavior aren't sustainable for long without impacting corporate culture. If people in the company refuse to recognize their own role in a dramatic organizational downturn, the company will soon find itself in receivership. In organizations that are fortunate—and whose change drivers have been astute and skillful—executives arrive at that realization with ample time to act on it. They understand that miracles will not necessarily be around the next corner, and that positive things only happen to those who are prepared to help themselves. They realize that the steps needed to reverse the situation must be taken not by others but by themselves. This means accepting change as inevitable and necessary. When enough people in the organization share this mindset, resistance to new initiatives begins to weaken. Only then do the first tentative explorations of a new reality take place, even as people are still adjusting to a sense of loss.

> *When enough people in the organization accept change as inevitable and necessary, resistance to new initiatives begins to weaken.*

Once the adjustments and reshuffling within the organization are complete, the next and final phase of the organizational change process (after turmoil and acceptance) is that people in the organization have to redefine themselves. After mourning the past, they have accepted the new way of doing things, recognized its advantages, and are now prepared to move forward collaboratively. They have internalized the new values and attitudes and have adopted a more positive attitude toward the future.

In an organization that hopes to steer this process of mourning and regeneration effectively, astute leadership is essential. Leaders must recognize that it takes time to relinquish the old and embark on the new, and that people facing organizational change (like those in personal change situations) need time to mourn the past. Effective leadership is a balancing act, especially during periods of change. Leadership, however, that instills vision and empowers and energizes its workforce effectively, must also take on a more "architectural" role in setting up the appropriate structures and control systems of the organization.

> *Leaders must recognize that it takes time to relinquish the old and embark on the new, and that people facing organizational change need time to mourn the past.*

Additional Factors Facilitating Change

After having highlighted the psychodynamics of individual and organizational transformation, a few observations concerning other factors that facilitate change can be added. From having assessed many successful change efforts, we have learned that there are two other factors in the process which influence the outcome of the transformation effort. The first is the presence of some kind of social support system to ease the process of change, and the second is the personality type of the individuals involved. Let us look at each of these factors in turn.

Social Support

People who experience a sense of isolation often find altering their behavior patterns more difficult. Without the support of their environment, they find their reluctance to change harder to overcome. Moreover, there appears to be a link between the existence of social support—that provides a crucial buffering function against stress—and good physical health. Indeed, social support is often the single most important factor in helping people to overcome the barriers to change. People seem to sense this intuitively: those who decide to embark on a journey of transformation often seek out people who can give them the support they need, whether instrumental or emotional.

> *Social support provides a crucial buffering function against stress ... and is often the single most important factor in helping people to overcome the barriers to change.*

Instrumental support tends to be task-directed, involving, for example, such things as assigning another pair of hands to a task that needs to be done; obtaining specialized outside assistance for a challenging project; providing authority along with responsibility; and, in short, handing over whatever resources are needed to make the change effort a success. Emotional support, on the other hand, is an essential way of maintaining and bolstering a person's self-esteem. This support may be given by a spouse, family member, friends, or colleagues at work—in effect, a network of people who offer reassurance, guidance, and an opportunity to share interests.

Sometimes, both forms of support issue from the same source. People in the process of change often seek out individuals who have experienced a similar situation. They do this partly to obtain practical help and advice, and partly to derive some consolation from not being the only one in that situation. In addition, the person who wants to change is motivated by the success of those who have already completed the process.

> *Making social support part of the corporate culture is essential during a transformation process, and it is a task that must start at the top.*

Making social support part of the corporate culture is thus essential during a transformation process, and it is a task that must start at the top. As we have said previously, the more effective leaders seem to have a considerable amount of emotional intelligence. Applying all they know about human behavior, they recognize the importance of providing a sense of security for their followers—a characteristic which could be described as the "teddy bear factor." Leaders who possess this "teddy bear factor" create trust and confidence by ensuring their employees know that genuine attention is being paid to them and that their concerns are being actively heard.

Locus of Control

From a personality perspective, some people possess a more internal locus of control, whereas others have a more external one. In other words, those with a mindset that's internally focused believe that they are in charge of their own lives; they perceive their destiny as governed by their own decisions, as opposed to outside factors. People with an internal locus of control recognize a strong relationship between their own actions and what happens around them. This secure self-belief, independence, and self-confidence makes these individuals less anxious. They tend to be more active in striving, and achieving, more future- and long-term-oriented, and more proactive and innovative (though less prone to engage in risky behavior). They are inclined to be more motivated and successful in life, both academically and professionally, than people with an external locus of control. Their self-control and strong belief in their own capabilities makes them resistant to influence, coercion, and manipulation.

An internal locus of control enables individuals to take charge of and maintain major personal change with greater ease and self-confidence. Their belief that they are in control of their own destiny prevents them from doubting the outcome of a self-initiated change process. With the sense that they are responsible for their own actions, they are aware that it is only themselves who can orchestrate their personal transformation. Once they have realized the necessity for change, they go ahead rather than waiting for some outside sign or agent to initiate it.

> *An internal locus of control enables individuals to take charge of and maintain major personal change with greater ease and self-confidence. ... People with an external locus of control, on the other hand, often see change as a threat.*

People with an external locus of control, on the other hand, often see change as a threat. Because they do not feel in control of the forces that affect their lives, they are prone to passivity, and unable to take decisive steps toward a personal transformation; this outlook makes them vulnerable to depression.

The Hardiness Factor

To continue the discussion of the influence of personality, the term "hardy personality" has been coined to describe people with an internal locus of control, however there is more to hardiness than simply feeling in control of life events. Hardy individuals feel a deep commitment to the activities in their lives: they are deeply curious, are eager to initiate new experiences, and perceive change as a positive challenge that will lead to further development. Hardy individuals have a strong commitment to self, an attitude of vigor, and a sense of meaningfulness. In contrast, non-hardy people feel victimized by events, and tend to view change as undesirable.

People who are considered to have a hardy personality possess affective, cognitive, and behavioral skills that make them better survivors in stressful situations. They have a feeling of control over what is happening to them, and are secure in themselves and thus are better able to tolerate ambiguity than others. As individuals, they think in a way that helps them to anticipate and internalize the changes they face. These people take charge; they make decisions; they feel that they are not at the mercy of events. They have a positive outlook on life and face its challenges with resilience, flexibility, and adaptiveness; consequently, they show greater job involvement than others and are happy to take on the role of catalyst. Not surprisingly, research indicates that innovative, proactive companies are largely composed of employees with an internal locus of control.

It is that same positive outlook that makes hardy individuals more stress-resistant than others, less prone to helplessness, depression, and physical illness; a commitment to self that helps them preserve their mental health under pressure. With an outlook characterized by a sense of control, commitment, and challenge, they have the skills to cope both psychologically and somatically with the stress caused by the change process.

> *We need to adapt to new circumstances when faced with the unpredictable, in the knowledge that winning life's battles is dependent largely on resilience.*

An individual's character traits—internal or external locus of control—and degree of hardiness are usually deeply ingrained and very difficult to influence. Companies subjected to a turbulent environment—those for whom change is the norm rather than the exception—would do well to select people who have a more internal locus of control. And it is their *reaction* to adversity, not adversity itself, that will determine how the company story will unfold.

We need to adapt to new circumstances when faced with the unpredictable, in the knowledge that winning life's battles is dependent largely on resilience, as the former US president Theodore Roosevelt said, "It is hard to fail, but it is worse never to have tried to succeed."[1]

---

[1] Theodore Roosevelt, speech at the Hamilton Club, Chicago (10 April 1899). *The Strenuous Life* (vol. 13 of The Works of Theodore Roosevelt, national ed., 1926), Chapter 1, p. 320.

13

The Holistic Picture: Culture and Organization

If I set the sun beside the moon,
And if I set the land beside the sea,
And if I set the flower beside the fruit,
And if I set the town beside the country,
And if I set the man beside the woman,
I suppose some fool would talk
About one being better.
—Gilbert Keith Chesterton

If we are to preserve culture, we must continue to create culture.
—Johan Huizinga

He who fights with monsters should see to it that he himself does not become a monster. And if you gaze long into an abyss, the abyss also gazes into you.
—Friedrich Nietzsche

Nobody

There is another Sufi story in which Nasruddin entered the royal reception area and sat on the most plush and ornate chair. The captain of the guards told him: "Please sit somewhere else, that chair is reserved for the most honorable guest."

"You think I'm an ordinary guest?" asked Nasruddin.

> "Are you an ambassador from a neighboring country?"
> "I'm much more important than that." Nasruddin responded.
> "Are you a minister?"
> "Much bigger than one."
> The guard became sarcastic, thinking he had accosted a fool. "I see, so you must be the King himself, your majesty," he said.
> "Higher than that!"
> "How dare you? Nobody is higher than the King!"
> "Precisely. I am nobody!" replied Nasruddin.

Executive coaching, when used effectively in an organization's leadership development portfolio, has many visible business outcomes, which include long-term improvements in personal and organizational effectiveness, whether measured by profit, cost-containment, or both. Arriving at this level of organizational change and transformation requires an executive coach who is experienced in transitioning fluidly between micro and macro levels. This is with the aim of contributing significantly to the success of a change process in the short term, and the creation of a self-sustaining coaching culture over the long term. Clearly, these change catalysts aren't a "nobody," but they should become one—given the fact that they want their clients to be in control over their own lives. They want them to be self-dependent.

As we have pointed out, change at the micro level can act as the starting point for an organization's macro developmental process. At this level, exploration and action planning is likely to focus on competencies, or performance coaching that includes how-to techniques, skill development, and attaining goals. Career transition or life coaching focuses on personal growth and career development. On a more advanced level, leadership/behavioral coaching is concerned with emotional intelligence or developing a more effective leadership style. Viewed at a micro level, leadership coaching can lead to an individual finding greater satisfaction at work and at home; it may result in lower stress levels, less frustration, and increased self-esteem and satisfaction in life. Consequently, coaching clients often achieve a greater sense of congruence between their public and private life; they can be seen to acquire a greater feeling of authenticity which is then reflected in the way they deal with their constituencies.

At the macro level, leadership group coaching has been seen to transform an organization's culture, structures, and patterns of decision-making, leading to an overall rejuvenation in workforce energy. By focusing on the underlying factors that contribute to the prevailing organizational culture, a long-term shift can be achieved, which, once understood, is like receiving the key to a secret code. Here, coaching for organizational and/or strategic change supports leaders as they introduce new change initiatives through a systemic orientation. Executive coaches guide organizational players as they explore aspects of organizational culture that may be enhancing or constraining creativity, productivity, and motivation. What we repeatedly emphasize is that attending to the micro undercurrents that determine an organization's macro culture is vital if change leaders are to succeed in any transformation effort.

> *Attending to the micro undercurrents that determine an organization's macro culture is vital if change leaders are to succeed in any transformation effort.*

Influencing an Organization's Culture

An organization's culture is comprised of the collective (conscious and unconscious) attitudes, beliefs, values, and behaviors that define "how things are done around here." Leaders set the tone, pace, and expectations for the culture and provide a defining example of what is expected, desired, and/or tolerated in the organization. Effective executive coaches can give a company the leverage to shift both organizational culture and individual behaviors by sensitizing its leadership to the unique dynamics of their organization.

The necessary transition from micro to macro—from a focus on the individual, through dyads and teams, to a systemic, organizational approach—is often the best method of engaging in an intervention, and this transition must be fluid and adaptive. The executive coach begins by conducting cultural audits through surveys, interviews, and/or focus group methods to establish a basis for cultural transformation. The corporate culture may be reframed as a set of values and behavioral patterns that should reflect an inclusive environment, and is respectful of diversity of thought, personality, lifestyle, and ethnicity. The ultimate aim may be to create a coaching culture throughout the organization that generates trust and mutual respect at all levels.

A coaching organization possesses an ambiance that actively encourages the kinds of behaviors and practices needed for continuous learning. It is founded on the exchange of both explicit and tacit knowledge, reciprocal coaching, and self-leadership development; this is all made visible in a culture that supports formal communication but also values informal open exchanges of information and knowledge. In such an organization, individuals feel free to discuss challenges and concerns and evaluate appropriate actions. In addition, a coaching culture contributes to a sense of mutual ownership, better networking, more effective leadership practices, and higher commitment, all laying the groundwork for better results across the organization.

Toward a Coaching Culture: A Case Example

Recently, a transformation was needed at a large European financial institution. One way of setting this process into motion was to design and implement a large-scale organizational coaching initiative. Their challenge was to guide the top executives of this financial institution as they made a valiant effort to transform the organization toward a coaching culture. The situation when they arrived was complex, and so they began by conducting a detailed organizational analysis.

> *A coaching organization possesses an ambiance that actively encourages the kinds of behaviors and practices needed for continuous learning.*

They quickly learned that, over the years, a macho culture (as the executives themselves described it) had infiltrated most of the organization, resulting in extremely risky moves that seemed to make little sense. Rogue traders had lost a significant amount of money, and the impact on the balance sheet had been aggravated by underperforming acquisitions. In addition, a very autocratic leadership cabal had stunted innovation and autonomy to the extent that people had settled into a dependency mode, having become unwilling or unable to propose or defend new ideas. Bankruptcy had become a real threat.

Deciding to take firm if radical action, the regulators of the country's central bank had instigated the dismissal of most of the senior executives and board members and brought in an outsider to stabilize the situation. The new CEO knew he needed to implement rapidly a major cultural change program. To eradicate a climate in which people looked the other way when irresponsible decisions were made, he wanted to encourage people to step forward and tell the truth. Transparency, open communication, mutual respect, honesty, and having a voice were to be central to this new environment. He also knew that the prevalent dependency culture was stifling personal and organizational growth. He wanted people to feel empowered and accountable for the sustainability and the future of the organization.

The first thing the coaching and consulting team did was to clarify that the old behavior patterns were, at best ineffective, and at worst, destructive. For example, they made it clear that macho behavior was no longer acceptable. In striving for exemplary leadership, they asked the senior group of executives to complete the Global Executive Leadership Mirror, a 360-degree leadership behavior questionnaire, which focuses on the charismatic and architectural roles of leaders, as well as the essential qualities of emotional intelligence, resilience to stress, and life balance. In addition, the executives were asked to complete a 360-degree personality test, which was *not* anonymous. The personality test looked at seven personality dimensions presented as polarities, such as self-esteem, assertiveness, conscientiousness, and adventurousness. Rather than forming the basis of a performance review, the executives' results on these tests were used to initiate discussion in a series of workshops called "The Leader Within." The data from these questionnaires and the interviews provided the coaching and consulting team with a starting point to tackle the difficult topic of individual and organizational change. For the individuals who completed these questionnaires the results functioned like a mirror, providing them with insights about developmental areas that they needed to work on to make themselves and the organization more effective.

The coaches and consultants, as part of The Leader Within workshops, would also present the participants with their current perceptions of their organization, engendering in them a sense of urgency and responsibility to make changes. Within a group setting (ten senior executives at a time), the coaching and consulting team helped them interpret their 360-degree feedback and, with the aid of the other participants, created for each of them a personal action plan. During these discussions they equipped participants with greater insight as to the danger associated with sticking to their old behavior patterns, and why the less frightening and liberating option was to adopt new behaviors.

As the participants recognized the need for change, the consulting and coaching team also provided hope, reassuring them that by developing the coaching culture they hoped to instill, they could support one another through the organizational transformation process. The team also ran a series of follow-up workshops that, acting cumulatively, created an iterative process of knowledge collection. To deepen the participants' understanding of their leadership style, another questionnaire (the Leadership Archetype Questionnaire) was used. The feedback from this second questionnaire provided a starting point not only to re-emphasize the importance of complementary leadership roles but also to encourage discussion as to the kind of cultural values needed to support their own vision of a successful bank. These additional seminars contributed to lively discussion of different organizational scenarios for the future.

The Leader Within and the follow-up workshops had a remarkable effect on participants. A highly defensive few who felt affronted by the coaching process eventually resigned or were asked to leave the bank, but the majority appreciated the benefits of contributing to a more open, transparent, and supportive culture. The top 50 who were most affected by the process initiated various initiatives, rolling out "The Leader Within" program to penetrate the lower levels of the organization. In addition, discussions about the future of the financial institution led to structural changes, including a different, more team-based reward structure where, among other things, executives' developmental efforts were also taken into consideration. Succession planning became more of a reality, and a senior line manager was appointed as the head of talent management reporting directly to the CEO.

> *When a coaching culture becomes part of the DNA of an organization, it means that an environment has been created where people feel able to express healthy disagreements with the boss; where people know that they have a voice; where there is transparency and trust; and where they feel sure that their opinions count.*

These workshops also contributed to a number of strategic initiatives, building on the core capabilities of this financial institution. While the workshops had an extraordinary effect on employee morale, the culture change was accompanied by a remarkable financial turnaround. The organization that had been on the brink of bankruptcy received a triple "A" rating from Moody's. Another gratifying side effect was that, because of its enlightened coaching practices, the reputation of the financial institution changed from being one of the worst places to work in the country to being an employer of choice.

This is a rather dramatic example of the multiple effects of introducing a coaching culture—and practices like continuous learning, knowledge exchange, reciprocal coaching, and self-leadership—can have on an organization. The "new" financial institution was characterized by relationships of trust, mutual respect, collaboration, insightful guidance, and a focus on assisting people to maximize their potential. The CEO, with the help of the team of executive coaches, was extremely successful at unlocking the creative, emotional, and entrepreneurial power of his people. That potential had always been there, but because of the previous poor leadership practices it had become dormant. As this story demonstrates, when a coaching culture becomes part of the DNA of an organization, it means that an environment has been created where people feel able to express healthy disagreements with the boss; where people know that they have a voice; where there is transparency and trust; and where they feel sure that their opinions count.

Bottom-Up and Top-Down

True cultural change comes about from a combination of both "bottom-up" and "top-down" leading and learning. Thus, coaching should be actively modeled at the top, teams should be supported by coaches, and people within the organization should be helped to develop their *own* skills as coaches.

But as has been made clear, this kind of group coaching work is not for the faint-hearted. If leadership coaches do not provide adequate, clearly understood value from the beginning, they will be quite rightfully terminated. Group oriented coaches must be people who can win the trust of even the most sceptical leaders and be able to engage the individuals and the whole group immediately. It goes without saying that those who are overly conscious of authority or sensitive to criticism will not find this kind of work attractive or satisfying.

> *If coaches do not provide adequate, clearly understood value from the beginning, they will be quite rightfully terminated.*

People interested in group coaching need to understand and to promote the conditions and behaviors required for change at the individual and the systems level. To engage in group coaching they need the ability to deduce rapidly the multiple levels of psychological dynamics occurring within the team and draw the most productive elements to the surface for conscious consideration. Also, they should subscribe to the motto "strike when the iron is hot," which refers to knowing when to remain quiet and when it is the right time to intervene. At any time, and something that the coaches are quite cognizant of, exciting reactions can come to the fore within each individual, between individuals in their personal relationships, within the group itself, and with respect to the various external forces influential to their thinking and operation. And this awareness of these manifold conscious and unconscious developments tends to be based on a deep theoretical and practical understanding of group dynamics and team developmental processes, as well as significant in-depth coaching experience with individuals and groups. However, that awareness is only as useful as the coach's ability to decide in the moment what really matters and how best to address it.

> *A coach's awareness of manifold conscious and unconscious developments in group coaching ... is only as useful as his or her ability to decide in the moment what really matters and how best to address it.*

Group coaches also require an awareness of the vicissitudes of power and its movement within groups, and, furthermore, feel comfortable intervening to redirect the way power is used in the group. They need to address the question of who has what kind of power and how are they using it?

Coaches also require the ability to put what they observe into simple, jargon-free language and the confidence to raise any issue with the team or its members at the right moment. Also, they must have a firm grasp of the ethical and practical dangers of working with a group and the individuals within it. In particular, leadership coaches should be aware of the consequences of being overly identified with one person (even if it is the CEO) or with any particular "side" to an issue. Thus, they have to possess the ability to remain neutral, respond appropriately, and intervene judiciously.

> *Coaches have to possess the ability to remain neutral, respond appropriately, and intervene judiciously.*

Finally, coaches require a keen sense of business acumen—of how businesses fundamentally make money. These are the executive coaches who will gain the trust of client leadership teams, not just because they know group and team processes, but also because they understand the business. They pay attention to the bottom line. In comparison, leadership coaches who do not know and understand the market conditions in a client's industry, the structure of the organization, and its competitive advantages, challenges, workforce, and organizational circumstances, are not credible as people who can assist the leadership team.

> *Leadership coaches who do not know and understand the market conditions in a client's industry, the structure of the organization, and its competitive advantages, challenges, workforce, and organizational circumstances, are not credible as people who can assist the leadership team.*

The Objectives of Organizational Coaching

The ultimate goal of our team interventions is to treat every coaching session—micro or macro—as one part of a holistic intervention that contributes in a small or significant way to transforming the cultural fabric of the entire organization. Organizations that foster a coaching culture demonstrate that they value their people by investing in their individual development within the organization. The objective of taking an organizational coaching approach is to create a culture where all members of the organization are able to engage in candid, respectful coaching conversations about how they can improve their working relationships and individual and collective work performance, unrestricted by hierarchical reporting relationships.

In organizational leadership coaching, all participants learn to value and use feedback as a powerful tool which, if employed wisely, can produce personal and professional development, high-trust working relationships, continually improving job performance, and ever-increasing customer satisfaction. To create a culture where employees have a voice and can make a difference ultimately improves the performance of the organization and its constituent parts. In our coaching work we have found that organizations that have coaching skills embedded in their culture are among the most successful.

> *An organization with a true coaching culture is one in which not only formal, prescribed leadership coaching occurs but also where most people use coaching behavior as a means of managing, influencing, and communicating with each other.*

An organization with a true coaching culture is one in which not only formal, prescribed leadership coaching occurs but also where most people use coaching behavior as a means of managing, influencing, and communicating with each other. These are the organizations that go one step further, integrating coaching modules into their leadership development as well as their general way of doing things. A coaching culture promotes more open communication and transparency, which in turn builds trust and mutual respect. Introducing coaching competencies into an organization is a powerful strategy and a means of actively cultivating a workplace that fosters learning and development. Not surprisingly, companies that are successful in this respect report significantly reduced staff turnover, increased productivity, and greater job satisfaction. The coaching model maximizes the resources of the organization, realigns relationships, and drives a focus on long-term strategy. These companies differentiate themselves by having a strong corporate identity and a committed workforce. All employees are aligned with the goals of the organization, and what is needed to get there. Creating a coaching culture helps leaders to think and plan more strategically, to manage risks more effectively, and to create and communicate vision and mission more clearly.

The more subtle interpersonal benefits of a coaching culture are manifested in the way individual employees perceive themselves and their world. It is an organizational culture that provides them with a sense of connection, inclusivity, and self-responsibility. In short, it makes them feel part of a whole and deters the sense of "us" and "them" that is a divisive but widespread culture in large hierarchical organizations. With the resultant sense of ownership in the organization, people move beyond the blame game and have the courage and right to speak their minds.

For a coaching culture to work, it has to be integrated into the wider business strategy, and, where this is not sufficient, powerholders may need to actively step forward as champions of change. Few innovative initiatives succeed without the support of senior executives who, if a coaching culture is to be successful, should be the first members to go through the process. If they are satisfied with the outcome, coaching is more likely to cascade throughout the organization and become part of its corporate fabric.

> *Few innovative initiatives succeed without the support of senior executives who, if a coaching culture is to be successful, should be the first members to go through the process.*

As we have set out, a coaching culture can be adopted in a number of different ways. Aside from group work, peer coaching is an example of a further dimension that can be introduced with a view to establishing relationships across the organization. The enhanced communication it encourages can be seen to support growth, encourage learning, aid problem solving, improve productivity, and enhance working conditions.

However, the introduction of a coaching culture to an organization raises the same challenges as any culture change programs. Therefore, it is important to examine all the costs and benefits and to anticipate, expect, and plan for resistance. It is not sufficient merely to announce the initiative, provide information, and assume that the change will take place—planning is essential.

> *The introduction of a coaching culture to an organization raises the same challenges as any culture change programs. Therefore, it is important to examine all the costs and benefits and to anticipate, expect, and plan for resistance.*

Benefits of Organizational Coaching as Indicated by Clients
Organizational coaching can:

- Enable the creation of a transitional space where people can express themselves frankly
- Unleash creativity and innovation
- Cultivate and promote an environment that delivers increased motivation and performance
- Create meaningful organizational cultural values
- Create a dynamic working environment that becomes a "best place to work"
- Make the organization the employer of choice
- Help organizations to achieve new strategic objectives
- Assist organizations in developing a portfolio of leadership talent
- Assist organizations in learning how to manage in a networking culture
- Help organizations become better at clarifying interconnections
- Identify healthy and neurotic organizational constellations
- Create a system for overseeing, mentoring, and supporting coaches throughout the organization
- Provide ongoing coaching training
- Implement a succession planning system
- Create an organizational framework that supports a coaching culture, clarifies roles, and guides the coaching
- Help organizations understand the interconnectedness that is the heart of a coaching culture

- Help companies involved in mergers and acquisitions navigate a new culture, integrate new teams, and align divisions
- Create a true learning organization where knowledge is shared, reducing errors and cycle time.

A Socratic Method of Leadership Coaching

The role of the group coach is to bring team members together to discuss their individual profiles and help them in finding ways to work as a whole. For example, if Eva knows that David is shy, she'll have a better appreciation of why he prefers to do tasks independently. Rather than concluding he's simply not interested in working with her, Eva can focus instead on finding ways to relate to David on his terms. Likewise, when David realizes that social acceptance is important to Eva, he can try to be more friendly and interested in what she's doing. With a greater level of understanding, team members begin to view one another differently. They learn to interpret the behavior of others with more insight and empathy and adjust their own behavior accordingly.

> *Developing a clear set of expectations concerning behavior and communications is an important aspect of team coaching that ensures one individual's preferences aren't given more importance than those of the team.*

This is why developing a clear set of expectations concerning behavior and communications is an important aspect of team coaching that ensures one individual's preferences aren't given more importance than those of the team. A great way to formalize some of these expectations is by writing a kind of informal "contract" that sets out the rules everyone is expected to follow and support. Treating each person with respect, offering opinions when needed, and talking directly to them when issues arise are all examples of ground rules that a team can use. Quite often, people have competing values, which, left unchecked, can be a major obstacle to team unity and effectiveness. For example, there will be inevitable problems when personal achievement is given higher priority than team performance. Yet, it's not uncommon for an organization to promote teamwork but still reward individual behavior.

13 The Holistic Picture: Culture and Organization

> *There will be inevitable problems when personal achievement is given higher priority than team performance. Yet, it's not uncommon for an organization to promote teamwork but still reward individual behavior.*

With cross-functional teams, departmental or business unit loyalties often get in the way of effective teamwork. When the personal goals of team members don't match those of the team, this can lead to "secret," hidden behavior patterns. As a group coach, the challenge is to identify the sources of competing values and find ways to fix them. Group coaching to improve team performance can necessitate different approaches for different teams and different people. What works for one team may not necessarily work for another. Effective working relationships are built by understanding team members' needs, preferences, and styles of work. By helping people understand their own styles and appreciate those of others, a group coach can work with them to change their behaviors and fully harness individual strengths. The outcome of a successful intervention should be a group of people who share a common purpose and have a clear direction. There will be a mutual understanding of roles, dependencies, and values, plus a strong relationship with stakeholders outside the team.

> *The outcome of a successful intervention should be a group of people who share a common purpose and have a clear direction.*

Naturally, the process of improving team performance takes time, and it may involve looking deeper than into team processes. Organizational systems—such as reward and recognition, performance management, and training—may also need to be addressed. However, the end result of this work is usually well worth it, because, when an organization supports its executives through leadership coaching programs, as in the bank example we described earlier, it is with a view to improving collaboration and communication across the organization as a whole. That said, executive coaching can also be considered an individual journey, where participants explore how to become more successful at managing their day-to-day responsibilities, meeting their goals, recognizing when they find themselves at crossroads, and, most importantly, creating a fulfilling life. By encouraging self-awareness of both conscious and unconscious behavior, the coach can help people acquire greater insight into knotty personal and organizational problems.

How does this work in practice? As noted before, in our practice we take a Socratic approach to leadership coaching, which we believe is more an art of discovery than delivery. The Socratic quality of leadership coaching involves asking a series of questions about a central issue and trying to find satisfactory answers through dialogue. The use of questions and conversation implies that a leadership coach begins from a position of humility and curiosity, not one of authority and knowledge.

> *Although coaching interventions are therapeutic, they are not therapy.*

The Socratic coach is a guiding figure, who respects and draws upon the experience and knowledge of the coaching client. Although coaching interventions are therapeutic, they are not therapy. Effective leadership coaches are aware of—and respect—the (often subtle) boundaries between coaching and psychotherapy, always with the guiding philosophy of "do no harm." Leadership coaches act as a mirror; they help people work out what they want, what they are good at, what they are not so good at, and where and how they can improve. They provide their clients with a safe transitional space in which they can explore fresh perspectives and have the trust to tackle any ordinarily "undiscussables." Confronting such issues is frequently seen to open new, highly productive dialogues, and unblocks the decision-making process.

Leadership coaches do not necessarily provide answers to problems but facilitate productive discussion around and exploration of potential solutions. They are not necessarily career advisors, consultants, mentors, or trainers, but give the kind of guidance that encourages individuals toward an understanding of their own strengths, weaknesses, desires, and fears. They partner with clients in a thought-provoking and creative way that inspires them to explore organizational leadership effectiveness and personal life satisfaction. The coach offers support to enhance skills, resources, and creativity that the client has been only subliminally aware of and helps people prepare for and adapt to change with a renewed commitment to self-development and achievement.

> *The coach offers support to enhance skills, resources, and creativity that the client has been only subliminally aware of and helps people prepare for and adapt to change with a renewed commitment to self-development and achievement.*

The Socratic coaching approach creates impact by expanding executives' communication skills and helping them to cultivate a more authentic leadership style. Effective coaches assist executives in developing cognitive agility, emotional capacities, motivation, skills, knowledge, and expertise. They support executives as they fine-tune their goals and strategies, challenge and reassess their assumptions, and align followers to the organization's goals. Through a more developed emotional intelligence, executives will then learn to consider the impact they have on others. Leadership coaches also encourage effectiveness in team and organizational culture management. Furthermore, leadership coaches assist executives in contextualizing and taking responsibility for their own career development and lifelong learning.

Assessing the Effectiveness of the Interventions

As guardians of leadership development, leadership coaches/consultants should also regularly assess, and learn from, previous organizational coaching initiatives. This is not an easy task, because organizational leaders rarely evaluate the effectiveness or impact of coaching aspects of leadership development programs. However, before proceeding with any large-scale coaching initiative, it is important to have a good understanding of the current state of affairs and what has to be accomplished.

It is not uncommon for leadership coaches to initiate sizeable practices and change initiatives. These, however, are under the guidance of key organizational leaders. The growth of these practices is always well-intentioned but are necessarily detached from the organization's talent development strategy. It is therefore recommended that assessment of the effectiveness of the coaching program is designed to be part of this strategy. Assessors need to remember that while individual coaching may produce positive results within short periods of time, its effectiveness as a leadership development strategy can only be determined over the long term. Regular reviews of the process should question whether coaching is truly making a difference to organizational strategy and performance improvement.

It is not enough to ask the recipients of coaching services if they are satisfied. Frequently, executives report delight and pleasure with the process, yet fail to enact visible change in their practice. This does not mean that coaching efforts should be abandoned—an assessment of a particular coach or an isolated intervention is not a reliable barometer of coaching effectiveness—but only a true 360-degree evaluation, involving suppliers, superiors, clients, and coaches, will yield more accurate information about the organization's coaching investment. It is long-term results that count.

> *Our whole life, from birth to death, is a process of continuous learning.*

Some coaching/consulting firms arrive at impressive return on investment (ROI) statistics, but we have to use caution when establishing the expected ROI of a leadership coaching initiative. A qualitative assessment of coaching is problematic because so many factors can affect learning, performance, and results. Leadership coaching is a complex human activity in which many of the variables—the result of a complex, ever-shifting world—are impossible to control. It is very different from selling widgets and calculating profits. Still, in our practice, we work as part of an ongoing reiterative process of action planning and feedback which results in a cultural coaching experience that is truly collaborative. Most importantly, we subscribe to the idea that our whole life, from birth to death, is a process of continuous learning. This also includes helping people learn how to learn and pursue the wisdom of Xunzi's statement when he said, "Not having heard of it is not as good as having heard of it. Having heard of it is not as good as having seen it. Having seen it is not as good as knowing it. Knowing it is not as good as putting it into practice."[1]

---

[1] Xunzi was a Chinese philosopher of Confucianism. Source: Xunzi (2014/c. 310–238 BC). "The Achievements of the Ru." In *Xunzi: The Complete Text*. Trans. by Eric L. Hutton. Princeton, NJ: Princeton University Press, p. 64.

14

The Senior Executive "Recycling" Workshops

When even the brightest mind in our world has been trained up from childhood in a superstition of any kind, it will never be possible for that mind, in its maturity, to examine sincerely, dispassionately, and conscientiously any evidence or any circumstance which shall seem to cast a doubt upon the validity of that superstition. I doubt if I could do it myself.
—Mark Twain

It is better to grope in the dark and wade through a million errors to reach the Truth than to entrust oneself to someone who knows not that he knows not. Has a man ever learnt swimming by tying a stone to his neck? So let me go my own way even if it is the wrong one.
—Sudhir Kakar

Watch your words; they become your actions. Watch your actions; they become your habits. Watch your habits; they become your character. Watch your character; it will become your destiny. And that's not always good.
—Manfred Kets de Vries

The Young Man and the Old Man

There is this story of a young man who left his home in search of a teacher who might furnish him with wisdom. Along the way, he came across an old man sitting under a tree. He told the old man that he was looking for a teacher to gain wisdom and asked him where he could find such a person. The old man smiled as he recited the names of cities near and far where he might find what he was looking for. Having written down all these places, the young man thanked him and hurried on his way. He walked and walked, and walked some more …

Thirty years went by, and one day, waking suddenly from a dream, the man understood and hurried back to where the old man still sat. Seeing him again, the younger man asked him why he hadn't revealed himself all those years before. The old man responded that he wasn't ready then, and then he added, "now, you are!"

Open Enrollment

Working with executives, we've noted three important things about our readiness to change: first, that readiness is our greatest ally; second, that our readiness will fluctuate; and finally that, in team interventions, there will always be resistance. The same applies when we are dealing with groups of executives from different organizations—our open enrollment transformative workshops are based on the research conducted at INSEAD, where for many years I was responsible for a program called "The Challenge of Leadership: Creating Reflective Leaders." Later on, many workshops of a similar nature have been developed that have proved to be highly effective in helping people and organizations change. Usually, people apply to these non-company-specific workshops driven by a point of inertia, when they feel they have seemingly insoluble interpersonal dilemmas, negative feelings about themselves, or perceptions of the world and others that make self-fulfillment seem impossible. Typically, these dilemmas are not clearly articulated in the applicant's mind when they apply to the program. To be accepted on the program each participant has to complete a detailed application form, with many quite personal questions that inform the faculty's first assessment as to the suitability of a candidate. Given the nature of the questions, this can be seen as the initial phase of the program. In addition, each future participant, wherever they are located, is interviewed face-to-face or through Zoom, WhatsApp, or FaceTime to see if they have what it takes to go through this kind of workshop in which their "life" case study will be the main source of interpretive material. In these interviews the faculty look for traces of psychological mindedness, the capacity to be open and responsive, and a serious interest and commitment to understanding oneself better.

The workshop consists of three or four multi-day periods with breaks of approximately seven weeks in-between (with potential follow-ups, if later required). The expectation is that during each week the participants learn more about themselves, and agree on a "contract" outlining what they intend to work on while on the job and at home during the time they are away from the workshop. They then return to the workshop to reflect and deepen their understanding. Mutual coaching is integral to the design of the program, so the "homework" assignments are monitored both by the participants and by us.

Like many of our organizational interventions, the faculty tend to run these programs as a dyad, as they have found that a second person's insight allows for a fuller and more complete view of what happens in the group and serves to protect both faculty members from blind spots. In addition, having two facilitators in the workshop at all times gives each of them the opportunity to move in and out of active and passive observational modes. The interchange between the two workshop leaders also provides a model for the participants of ways of relating to each other and handling conflict. Furthermore, the participants are presented with a working example of collaborative work, making for a richer way of understanding complex human phenomena.

> *A person's narrative is considered a process of self-discovery wherein the other participants in the group can help them, through vicarious listening and comparisons with their own stories, to gain a better understanding of the problems they are currently facing, be it in their public or private lives.*

The basic material of the workshop is the "life" case study, although the first module is the most structured, with a number of short interactive lectures which consider high-performance organizations, organizational culture, leadership (exemplary and dysfunctional), the career life cycle, cross-cultural management, and organizational stress. The central model of psychological activity and organization for the workshops however always returns to the personal case history. Each participant will, at some stage during the workshop, volunteer to sit in the "hot seat." This is an extremely important part of the experience. As a person narrates his or her life story, experiences and actions become more organized. Their narrative is therefore a process of self-discovery wherein the other participants can help them, both through vicarious listening and comparisons with their own stories, to gain a better understanding of the problems they are currently facing, be it in their public or private lives.

During the second module, some time is devoted to the processing of a number of feedback instruments. A key part of this activity is the Global Executive Leadership Mirror, a 360-degree feedback instrument referred to earlier that was developed by KDVI, and which consists of 12 dimensions that have been seen to contribute to leadership effectiveness. In addition, a personality test is given—The Personality Audit—which delivers additional, in this case non-anonymous, feedback, provided by people from their public and private lives. Further information is also compiled from other family members and close friends so as to establish as objective a perspective as possible. This information is the basis for a more refined action plan in the interregnum between the second and third periods. In addition, another 360-degree feedback instrument may be used: the Leadership Archetype Questionnaire gives the person insights about his or her particular leadership style. However, the main focus of the third module is the consolidation of these acquired insights, the internalization of change, and future action plans.

Separate from the plenary sessions, the participants also spend a considerable amount of time in small groups in and outside the workshop facility. These interactions are extremely valuable as participants consolidate newly acquired behavior patterns. Eventually, the people in the workshop form an intense learning/coaching community whereby each participant offers feedback to others in a constructive way, in particular if they observe them falling back into behavior patterns that they are trying to unlearn. In fact, it may often be the case that, by the third week, many of the participants know each other better than many of their family members do. At this point, the interchange within the plenary session will have become extremely free flowing, with much less intervention needed by the facilitators. The group has turned into a self-analyzing, coaching community. Given the quality of their interventions, the members of the group demonstrate a remarkable level of emotional intelligence compared with the first week. In many instances there will be a follow-up session a year later (in some instances these follow-ups have occurred year after year), which offers the faculty an opportunity to assess the degree to which certain behavior patterns have become truly internalized.

A Bird's Eye View

> The cocktail party has this familiar artificial quality found on such occasions. There is the usual nervous laughter, the noise of glasses. People are milling around each other. They try to make contact. They try to make conversation. Quite a few of the people present are somewhat ill at ease. There is a certain amount of electricity in the air. What to talk about? How to relate to each

other? The topics range from recent political events, to travel, to cross-cultural anecdotes. Is this just another random encounter of a group of executives? True? Not really! In spite of appearances the cocktail party is carefully choreographed. There is a purpose behind the ritual. It is an awkward but necessary step to get the leadership workshop underway.

Participants have arrived from all over the globe. Now, they are trying to feel their way around. Specialists on group dynamics would say that this way of acting is part of the "being polite" group phase. The members of the group struggle with questions of inclusion and exclusion. The participants are trying to find out the background of the other members. Who has been selected on the program? What are the other participants like? What countries do they come from? Their behavior represents a snapshot in time, filled with excitement, but also with a certain degree of anxiety. A spectator from Mars, however, would be amused to see this gathering of so many captains of industry looking like fish out of water. For once, they aren't in control; for once, they don't really know what to expect. They are caught in a situation where they aren't the ones pulling the strings. For once, they aren't masters of the universe. There is nobody really to push around. Instead, they are anxiously testing the waters. They introduce themselves to each other. They engage in polite talk. Some don't really know how to position themselves. They feel quite awkward. Some cope with an uncomfortable situation by talking too much; others drink too much. At a subliminal level they are aware that, in contrast to the role they play in the office, it will be harder to hide behind a public self. It will not be as easy to keep their masks on. Formula-like statements will be more difficult to maintain. They are caught up in a totally unknown situation with all its specific fantasies and defensive reactions. Many thoughts race through their mind. Why didn't I stay at the office? Why did I leave familiar ground? There must be a better way to spend my time. What am I going to get out of all this? Isn't this all a waste of time? What am I doing here? What am I doing to myself?

Although word-of-mouth has, for many years, been the most powerful driver of executive applications, for a number of them, it all started when their VP Human Resources or another colleague gave them a brochure about the program. The description sounded quite interesting. The design aroused their curiosity, stimulated a fantasy. Some saw the workshop as an opportunity to do something different, to take a break from the routine of office life. Here was an opportunity to do something for themselves. They thought that perhaps the program could provide answers to some of the questions they had been asking themselves, questions relating to a sense of disquietude. Lately, life had lost much of its novelty. Their work didn't feel the same as it had in the past. That original sense of excitement and purpose was gone. Work had become too much of a routine. They felt stuck in a rut and rarely did anything new. They wondered what had happened to their original sense of discovery and curiosity. What had happened to their creativity? When was the last time they experienced that "Everest feeling"—that feeling of immersion, excitement, and total involvement? They had stopped being able to lose themselves in their activities. Instead, they seemed to be doing more of the same. Was it a midlife crisis?

It was something of a drag completing the rather complex admission form. It asked too many quite personal questions. It was a real pain to respond to all of them. Such forms were good for students, but at their level?! Some of these questions still puzzled them, questions that were quite different from the ones they would get from journalists or investment analysts. Who likes to write about things they were not good at? How should they respond when asked about risky things they had done in their life? Whatever irritation they had, the type of questions asked on the admissions form indicated that this was not going to be a traditional executive program. But if they were being honest with themselves, they didn't really want another traditional executive program. They had tried them all. As far as executive programs were concerned, they had reached the end of the road.

Then there was the interview. Out of the blue, there was this person, apparently the workshop leader, asking them bizarre questions. Asking why he should give him or her a place in the program. What would they contribute? Asking what complaints their significant other had about them? What kind of things made them angry? What made them happy? Did they have repetitive dreams, even nightmares? Whose business was it to ask questions about wild fantasies? What had all that to do with becoming more effective as a leader? Strangely enough, when asked at the end of the interview if they still wanted a place in the program, they had given an affirmative response. In some ways the workshop had really begun!

After the cocktail party, like most other executive workshops, they were given a short introduction describing the daily workshop schedule, followed by a dinner. That took care of the initial formalities. There was a last chance for polite dinner conversation. But they all knew that it was the quiet before the storm.

The next day the workshop started in earnest. At the announced opening time anxiety was high, people appeared apprehensive, looking expectantly at the workshop leader. He gave a short lecture on emotional intelligence and irrational behavior in organizations. He made some comments about effective and dysfunctional leadership. Then he reiterated the basic premise of the workshop, that it was to be fueled by the "life" case study. Case presentations were going to be the main learning tool. He mentioned that each life case study would present a unique situation that would contribute to the learning process. He also mentioned that there could be "no interpretation without association," the implication being that each participant would get as much out of the workshop as he or she put into it. Dreams were also welcome. The workshop leader made it clear that he had spoken to all participants, who all had accepted the ground rules to work on a number of significant problems, business or private, that needed resolution.

From then on, the workshop was on its way. How the various participants would handle their emerging anxiety would depend on their personality structure, their historic defense mechanisms, and the specific dynamics that evolved in the group. The immediate behavioral data would be used to explore conscious and unconscious material, and defensive operations. With that, let the first life case study begin!

A Personal Interlude

As consultants and coaches we have been striving for many years to find the best "format" that would foster the change process in senior executives. We have tried to deal with the question of how to help senior executives to become more effective, be it at work or at home. We wanted to establish what would get them out of the rut? What could be done to help them reinvent themselves?

Steeped in the psychodynamic-systemic/clinical tradition, we are familiar with the fact that, according to psychoanalysts, the route to insight and lasting change may be a lengthy treatment procedure involving anywhere from two to five sessions a week. Needless to say, the prospect of such a monumental undertaking would not be very attractive to senior executives who have neither the time nor patience to engage in such an activity. Furthermore, as many of these people tend to be quite self-centered, they have a very short attention span. Our challenge became to work successfully with a group of people who all think they are the center of the universe. To be able to do this we had to find a more time-effective way of reaching them. We needed a procedure that would grab the attention of a group of highly self-centered people. And we had to get that attention fast, early in the first week, otherwise they would not hang around.

> *Our challenge became to work successfully with a group of people who all think they are the center of the universe.*

Our challenge, as indicated in the previous chapters, became to develop a method of intervention that would accelerate and condense the more traditional therapeutic processes, while remaining true to basic clinical principles. We had to find a less traditional way to overcome resistances to change and to confront issues that were often out-of-awareness problems of a preconscious and unconscious nature. We had to mobilize in an effective way unconscious mental processes to achieve positive results. In addition, the challenge was to create changes in behavior patterns that wouldn't turn out to be "flights into health" or transient "highs," as is so often the case with the miracle "cures" offered by so many psychological snake-skin salespeople. The question became what conceptualizations and settings could we use to jump start the change process?

> *The challenge was to create changes in behavior patterns that wouldn't turn out to be "flights into health" or transient "highs," as is so often the case with the miracle "cures" offered by so many psychological snake-skin salespeople.*

Given our clinical orientation, that jump start of the change process emerged with the help of experiments carried out in short-term dynamic psychotherapy. As noted in Chapter 2, this therapeutic approach offers a different avenue to help people acquire insight into the role life events and ongoing experiences play in perpetuating their problems, and to do so faster. Therapists have discovered that focused interventions of a more direct nature (combined with a solid dose of empathy and psychological support) frequently resulted in remarkable improvements to the mental state of the individuals concerned. Clarification of defensive reactions—whereby a problem is analyzed more closely and brought into sharper focus—also appeared to contribute to a change in behavior. By engaging in these activities, the presenting problem would be made more explicit so that the person whose life situation was being discussed acquired a greater awareness of the psychological forces influencing his or her behavior.

After experimenting with short-term dynamic psychotherapy in one-to-one encounters with executives (with a modest degree of success), with the objective being to increase their effectiveness in their organizations, we realized that more was needed to create lasting change in their behavior patterns. Simple one-to-one coaching had only limited results. We needed to increase the discomfort zone of the participants. We discovered that if we could create a situation of high intensity and total involvement through the creation of a learning community—whereby each member had a stake in creating a corrective emotional experience for others—there was the possibility that the change process could be further accelerated. We saw that to facilitate these changes, we needed to create some kind of "transitional space," a space in which participants, protected from the reality of the outside world, could safely experiment with new forms of interacting.

After a great deal of trial and error, we conceived that we could create an intense learning community by combining some of the methods used in short-term dynamic psychotherapy with the interventions derived from group dynamics, with additional concepts derived from organizational, leadership, and other theories. In using the most effective principles of these various theories, we were able to set the stage for a more concentrated change effort.

What can executives expect when they go on this journey? What is this process all about? How do people change? "To own your own life," what obstacles does a person have to go through, and what will best facilitate their journey?

> *A major precondition for change is a willingness to change.*

Taking the Road Less Traveled

A major precondition for change is a willingness to change. To be able to change you have to be motivated. Certain conditions have to be met, however, in order to take this kind of journey. Careful selection is in order—only relatively healthy people have the psychological strength to participate in this type of intensive seminar. Not everyone has the personality make-up to participate. What are some of these preconditions? What are some of the selection criteria?

If you decide "to own your own life," you have to ask yourself, what is your level of motivation? Are you prepared to take a hard look at yourself? Are you willing to do the work? Or are you merely looking for a quick fix or a magic pill that will take care of all your problems? Do you have the capacity to be open and responsive? If you decide to take this journey of self-discovery, are you willing or able to open up to others?

This brings us to the ability to establish relationships. Do you have what it takes for human connectedness? Do you have the ability and willingness to engage in meaningful emotional interaction? Having the capacity to talk about very personal thoughts and feelings makes the change process considerably easier. Experience tells us that people who have a history of give-and-take with a number of significant people in their lives are more likely to change. Hermits, please don't apply for this kind of program!

> *People who have a history of give-and-take with a number of significant people in their lives are more likely to change.*

The way you manage emotions is another factor that indicates a receptivity to change. Can you tolerate the anxiety that comes with putting yourself in a more vulnerable position? How do you experience your emotional life? Is it very passionate? Or are your emotional experiences rather flat? When other people talk about their life's ups and downs, do these incidents touch you? Are you one of these people with tears in their eyes during a very emotional scene in a dark movie theater?

Psychological mindedness is another factor that needs to be taken into consideration in the change equation. Are you somewhat curious about your inner life? Do you like to learn more about yourself? Would you like to know why you behave the way you do? Can you look beneath the surface and grasp the emotional meaning of maladaptive behavior? Can you verbalize your thoughts, feelings, fantasies, and inner personal life? Do you have the capacity for introspection? In understanding another change facilitator, the Danish philosopher Søren Kierkegaard's statement—"It is quite true what philosophy says: that life must be understood backwards. But then one forgets the other principle: that it must be lived forwards"[1]—becomes relevant. Do you have the ability to recognize how your patterns of interaction are integrated and related to past experiences? Understanding the connection between past and present becomes an important variable in the change equation.

Finally, your responses to observations by others about your behavior become relevant. Are you receptive to interpretations by others, or do you become defensive? Do you understand what other people are trying to tell you? Finally, the flexibility of how you react to certain stressful interventions, and the appropriateness of your reactions, becomes another indicator of your receptivity to change.

---

[1] Søren Kierkegaard (1996/1843). "Entry of Journal IV A 164." In *Søren Kierkegaard. Papers and Journals: A Selection.* Trans. Alistair Hannay. Harmondsworth, UK: Penguin.

A Case Example

One CEO started his presentation, making a number of the other executives highly uncomfortable—after all, the workshop had only just started, and they expected to hear about knotty business problems. Instead, he created this sense of discomfort by declaring that he was an unwanted child, an accident, an unexpected addition to parents who already had four sons. To take care of another son was the last thing they had in mind. All throughout his childhood, his mother made her disappointment about his unexpected arrival quite clear. If they had planned for another child, they would have liked it to be a daughter. The executive, in his presentation, expressed his sadness about his mother's comments and explained how his mother's attitude had very much been the story of his life. The theme of being unwanted had always haunted him. He also mentioned his father, a person who wasn't very present. He worked long hours as a specialist in internal medicine at a local hospital. And if he was around, he remained quite distant. It was extremely difficult to get his attention. He mentioned how competitive he had been in fighting for his father's attention. His brothers had to bear the brunt of this. He told a funny story about how he once succeeded in shifting blame to one of his brothers for a dent in the family car—something that had really been his doing. He mentioned, as an aside, that he had always been very good at shifting responsibility and letting others take the blame.

This individual realized that a major theme in his life was proving that he was worth having around; that he counted for something. To get his parents' attention he had excelled in school. He had also been very good at sports. But he emphasized that he wasn't just a teacher's pet. There was another side to him—a rebellious streak that wasn't always so obvious. While talking about this, he mentioned the many girls in his life as a teenager and afterwards.

After graduation, he had chosen engineering as his field of studies, largely to impress his father. Computer science had been his specialty and after obtaining his engineering degree he decided to find a job in the industry. That was also the time of his failed marriage and the birth of his son. After an uphill struggle, he had become the CEO of a very successful software company.

According to him, people in his company either loved or hated him. As he set extremely high standards for himself, he could be a very hard taskmaster to others. The result was that he had lost a number of very capable executives. The latest departure (a woman with high potential) had irritated his non-executive chairman who strongly suggested that he needed to work on his leadership style. At the time he had listened to the chairman's comment, but had done nothing about it. What really got him started thinking about his life was the news that he had colon cancer, which, fortunately, was operated on in time. As a close family member had previously died of colon cancer, this discovery had given him a real scare. Deciding to come on this workshop had been a response to the convergence of these events.

This person's frankness about his life so very early in the program loosened up the group. Many were touched by the intensity with which he described his experiences. Because of the strength of his presentation, he made it easy for others to visualize what he had gone through. Many of the themes he touched upon echoed themes in their own lives and brought up a host of their own memories.

From his story it became quite clear that this was a person who was highly motivated to do something about his present situation. He had realized that his personal life was a mess. He also recognized that he had to work on his leadership style. He was aware that to go on as before was not an appealing option. In presenting his problems he expressed a considerable amount of emotion—to the point of having tears in his eyes. From the little we had learnt of him already, human connectedness didn't seem to be a problem. In spite of him being a hard taskmaster in the office, he related well to most people. Nor was psychological mindedness an issue—he was very interested in understanding himself better. In questioning, it was clear that he was able to make connections between his present behavior and past experiences, and he seemed to be ready to take the jump and try to change some of his behavior patterns.

> *At the heart of our practice is a deep interest in the riddle that, if the human tendency is to resist change, how does the process of change ever get underway?*

The Drivers of Change Revisited

At the heart of our practice is a deep interest in the riddle that, if the human tendency is to resist change, how does the process of change ever get underway? What is it that causes a person's resistance to weaken? Revisiting the model of personal transformation, we saw in the case of this CEO that a strong inducement in the form of pain or distress had been required to initiate the change motion—a level of discomfort that outweighed the pleasure of "secondary gains" (psychological benefits such as sympathy and attention).

To be open to change, people must experience a sense of concern about their present situation; this might be triggered by family tensions, health problems, negative social sanctions, an accident, feelings of isolation leading to a sense of helplessness and insecurity, problem behavior at work, distressing incidents happening to someone close, or the weight of the cumulative hassles and frustrations of daily life. The CEO in our example had finally gained the motivation to do something about his life, recognizing that he would end up a very lonely person if he continued the way he was.

> *To be open to change, people must experience a sense of concern about their present situation.*

As mentioned in the chapter about personal transformation (Chapter 9), people who have undergone major internal change confirm that a high level of unpleasant emotion (anxiety, anger, sadness, or frustration, for example) occurs in the period prior to change, generally precipitated by a stressor such as one of those listed above. This negative emotion raises their awareness of the serious negative consequences of continuing their dysfunctional behavior patterns, making the status quo increasingly difficult to maintain. As in this case example, this person clearly recognized that neither the passage of time nor minor changes in behavior would improve the situation—indeed, the situation would likely to become even worse if nothing drastic was done. Even this insight, however, wouldn't automatically compel him to act, but it did set in motion a mental process whereby he was able to consider alternatives. This wish for redress can turn into one of the engines of change. Although initially every other unfamiliar situation appears more frightening than the status quo, a preferable alternative to the stalemate may begin to emerge. The hurdles might still seem insurmountable, but a goal is in sight. Accepting the need for change is a necessary first step, but on its own it is no guarantee of action. People need a push in the form of what we have earlier described as a "focal event"—a crisis. In this case, the other participants in the workshop gave him the push that he needed, but the main "push" had happened in the form of his cancer scare. It served as a wake-up call that he needed to reevaluate his lifestyle.

> *To be able to change it is necessary to describe what we'd like to change. A focus needs to be established and focal problem identified.*

Of course, to be able to change it is necessary to describe what we'd like to change. A focus needs to be established and focal problem identified. If there is no clear agenda and explicit goals it is difficult to assess progress. Fortunately, listening to a person's history we often find a thin red line that began in the past and continues throughout their life. The challenge is to identify this thin red line and clarify what role it plays in a person's *present* actions. This means listening carefully to their story and engaging in a process we call sense making.

> *Listening to a person's history we often find a thin red line that began in the past and continues throughout their life. The challenge is to identify this thin red line and clarify what role it plays in a person's present actions.*

More often than not, the stories we tell about ourselves have to do with seemingly insoluble dilemmas, a negative self-concept, or a misguided perception of the world and of others that contribute to a state of unhappiness, a lack of fulfillment, and which can add to problems at work. These dilemmas, however, are not yet clearly conceptualized in the person's mind. They are often preconscious and thus only vaguely experienced. What the person feels more keenly are various mixtures of helplessness and hopelessness. At this point the challenge then becomes how to arrive at greater specificity. Agreement needs to be reached by the people in the "hot" seat and the "audience" that a specific dilemma or dilemmas that arise during the life case presentation needs working on. This will be the basis for a "contract" between the person and the rest of the group. But first, the major life themes need to be identified—and dealt with. Here we always keep in mind the words of the Roman philosopher Seneca: "Men do not care how nobly they live, but only how long, although it is within the reach of every man to live nobly, but within no man's power to live long."[2]

> *More often than not, the stories we tell about ourselves have to do with seemingly insoluble dilemmas, a negative self-concept, or a misguided perception of the world and of others that contribute to a state of unhappiness, a lack of fulfillment, and which can add to problems at work.*

---

[2] Seneca (1925/c. 65 AD). "Letter XXII: On the futility of half-way measures." In *Seneca: Ad lucilium epistulae morales*. Trans. Richard M. Gummere. London: William Heinemann, line 17.

15

Major Life Themes

The man who is not satisfied with little, is satisfied with nothing.
—Epicurus

Be not grieved (at its loss), for He will give (thee) a hundred such (gifts) in return.
—Jalálu'ddín Rúmí

From childhood's hour I have not been
As others were—I have not seen
As others saw—I could not bring
My passions from a common spring—
From the same source I have not taken
My sorrow—I could not awaken
My heart to joy at the same tone—
And all I lov'd—I lov'd alone— …
—Edgar Allan Poe

A Sign for Prosperity

There is a Zen story of a shop owner who wanted a sign to put up in front of his shop that would bring him good luck and many customers. He asked a Zen master to write something down that could encourage the prosperity of his family for years to come. It would be something that the family could cherish for generations. The Zen master agreed to do so but said that it would take him at least a day. He told the shop owner to return the next evening, and the sign should be ready.

The next day when the shop owner returned, he saw the sign that the Zen master had written, but was horrified at the message. It read, "Grandfather dies, Father dies, Son dies."

Angrily, the shop owner said to the Zen master, "I asked you to write something down that could bring happiness and prosperity to my family. Why do you give me something depressing like this?"

The Zen master said, "This is not an evil curse. If your son should die before you, this would bring unbearable grief to your family. If your grandson should die before your son, this also would bring great sorrow. Therefore, no son should die until both his grandfather and his father have passed away before him. This is the natural order of things, and therefore it is not an evil curse, but a great blessing for your family. This is true happiness and prosperity."

The Haunting Questions

Looking back at the thousands of executives that have undergone executive coaching with us, a number of major life themes emerge. For the purpose of sense making, it is essential that these themes are recognized so that frames of understanding and interpretation can be formulated. At the same time, we recognize that sense making isn't always easy. After all, there are vast amounts of information to process. And while the events in our lives tend to happen in a certain sequence in time, their significance to ourselves can be based on our own order and be part of a continuous thread of revelation.

> *Events in our lives tend to happen in a certain sequence in time, yet their significance to ourselves can be based on our own order and be part of a continuous thread of revelation.*

Loss

One theme can be summarized as loss, be it past, present, or impending. From the stories we hear, this is one of the most difficult things to deal with. Regardless of the form that loss takes, its depressive consequences may linger for months or even years as the person grieves what might have been, and over the poor hand of cards he or she has been dealt. The most dramatic example, and the one with enormous repercussions in our lives, is the loss of an important figure, whether through separation, divorce, or death. Another form of loss that is profoundly significant is that of our health and well-being through illness, or a physical disability.

Turning to the world of work, the loss of a job can have wider implications, such as the loss of the community the person used to belong to. Career setbacks such as a demotion or retirement can also be experienced as loss. Often what is at play here is an imbalance between career expectations and actual achievement. People may have reached a point in their career when they are wondering if the "dream" they had sustained regarding career success will ever be fulfilled. Are they ever going to be the CEO of the company? Are they going to be a member of the board? What can be done now to achieve their career goals? How can they cope with the encroaching disappointment?

> *People need to be encouraged to look for opportunities and discover that there are alternatives; that there can be new beginnings.*

Any of these forms of loss may linger on, with consequences such as panic attacks or depressive reactions. In many instances, the person is grieving what could (or should) have been, and if they've been given the short straw in life. The challenge is to help them break out of this depressive cycle and reframe the situation, giving them a more hopeful outlook on life. People need to be encouraged to look for opportunities and discover that there are alternatives; that there can be new beginnings.

Interpersonal Conflict

Another area of difficulty that can be a catalyst for enrolling in a leadership coaching workshop is the intensification of an interpersonal conflict. This kind of conflict can occur in the context of a more intimate relationship within the family or with friends. It might also concern disputes between work colleagues. In one example, an executive described the stress of an ongoing battle with one of the non-executive members of his board—he was enlisting the help of the group to find a constructive solution out of his current impasse. Another senior executive of a family business was trying to find new ways to break a long-standing feud with one of his brothers concerning the future direction of the company. A further example involves a CEO caught up in a merger process who sought ways to solve a culture (organizational and cross-cultural) incompatibility problem with the executives of the other company.

In the case of personal relationships, disputes frequently develop when two people have nonreciprocal expectations about their interaction. Specifically, these can take the form of a marital dispute, conflict between parents and children, or extended family or friendship network. Often at the core of these problems is a lack of interpersonal competencies—we frequently see executives who have trouble initiating relationships because they lack the repertoire of social skills. Some are able to start relationships but lack the ability to sustain them when it comes to true commitment, intimacy, and expectations of fidelity and loyalty.

Boredom

Relating to the domain of work, boredom can have underestimated implications for those who find their job satisfaction progressively diminishing. Quite a number of the participants in the workshops present with this problem, and have exemplified the dire consequences not only for their mental health (i.e., suffering from depressive symptoms) but also the health of their organization. One participant explained how, in a bid to fight his boredom, he had engaged in a disastrous acquisition spree. It was his way of feeling excited and alive … until the financials caught up with him. As a result of the dramatic drop in share price, he was asked by his board of directors to resign. He explained that one of the reasons he had enrolled in the workshop was to find ways to renew himself without becoming destructive to his organization.

> *Relating to the domain of work, boredom can have underestimated implications for those who find their job satisfaction progressively diminishing.*

Addictions

At times, the thin red line that determines the specific problem area is of a more symptomatic nature. In such instances, identification of the problem can be easier. Although some of these problems are not really brought up during the plenary session, and more likely will be discussed in the smaller groups, the range of potential symptoms is enormous—from habit disorders, numerous phobias, and frequently alcohol or drug problems.

Others may have a sexual addiction problem—an issue that they will be quite reluctant to admit. Some people may have phobias of public speaking or anxiety in social situations. They fear the scrutiny of others and are anxious about acting in a way that will be humiliating or embarrassing when they are in such situations. The inability to sleep (insomnia) is another example of a specific problem, as is the fear of being in airplanes. The origin for having these symptoms varies. Many of these symptomatic problems, however, are triggered by frightening experiences that once happened but have been forgotten. Whatever the origin, these symptoms can become so severe that they interfere with day-to-day functioning and become a significant source of distress.

> *Many symptomatic problems are triggered by frightening experiences that once happened but have been forgotten.*

Developmental Imbalance

Another issue that regularly emerges concerns situations of developmental imbalance, meaning that certain expectations about life remain unfulfilled. The previously mentioned imbalance between career expectation and reality is a good example. More important, however, is a more holistic developmental imbalance. As we get older, we may be faced with life changes that necessitate moving from one social role to another, and some people struggle with taking on this new role. A good example of a developmental imbalance is when people realize that everybody at their age has a committed relationship but that this event seems to have passed them by. It may contribute to an increasing sense of loneliness. What adds to this sense of loneliness could be the desire to have children. People who fail to cope adequately with these transitions often experience role change as a loss that can contribute to depressive reactions. The workshop may help them discover that a logical way of coping is reaching out, establishing new connections, exploring new relationships.

For example, the issue of a developmental imbalance was pointed out to one executive during one of the leadership workshops. This executive repeatedly referred to his terrific relationship with his girlfriend. He went on at great length explaining what a good time they had together. Yet, after some questioning, it became clear that this relationship had been going on for more than 10 years and that the girlfriend was becoming increasingly exasperated by his lack of commitment. The other participants learned that a previous girlfriend had eventually given up on him. During the discussion, the problems he experienced with commitment became increasingly clear. The marriage of his parents had ended in a painful divorce, a factor (after some questioning) that seemed to play a role in his unwillingness to take the next step with his girlfriend. At the same time, he described his pleasure in playing with the children of his brother and how he had become their favorite uncle. His lack of commitment was not only related to his private life, it spilled over in his life at the office. Making decisions didn't come easy to him. He was a great procrastinator. Others had to push him to decide on closure. Although he was now running the show at the office, this pattern of behaving and acting had also delayed his career progression.

Life Balance

Life balance is an inevitable theme that continues to reoccur in the presentations of most senior executives. As life passes and children grow up, many of these people perceive that they are leading a mortgaged life. Finding time for the family becomes more and more of an uphill battle and many sense they're missing out on quality time with their children. They aren't present at the important moments in their children's lives. Eventually, they may even become estranged from them. At the same time, they are prisoners of their own ambitions. They like to be on the fast track but feel guilty about what it means for the family. One reason that they signed up for a workshop is that they are looking for ways to rearrange their priorities. In search of a better balance, they are desperate for advice. One CEO found himself alone with his 7-year-old daughter and discovered that he had nothing to say. She had become like a stranger to him. This became a turning point in his life.

The Primacy of Meaning

Lastly, but most importantly, many of the executives in the leadership workshop raise questions about meaning. What can they do to give their life more meaning? Often belatedly, they realize the importance of the words of the Swiss psychiatrist Carl Jung: "The least of things with a meaning is worth more in life than the greatest of things without it."[1]

---

[1] Carl Jung (1933). *Modern Man in Search of a Soul*. Trans. W.S. Dell and C.F. Baynes. London: Kegan Paul, Trench, Trubner & Co.

For some, the search for meaning may have been a theme all through their career. For others, with aging, it has become more pressing. After having been very successful in their career, some may have the urge to give something back, but wonder how to go about it. From there, various questions emerge. Can this search for meaning be achieved within the context of work? Or do activities outside work have to be found to give this kind of gratification? How can they have the biggest impact? What can they do that is most suitable given their personality make-up?

> *Humans are said to be unique in that we adapt and run our lives in full knowledge not only of beginnings but also of endings.*

The Stealth Motivator

Humans are said to be unique in that we adapt and run our lives in full knowledge not only of beginnings but also of endings. But our anxiety about death causes a great degree of conscious or unconscious discomfort that manifests itself in a wide variety of affective, cognitive, developmental, and sociocultural reactions. How we metabolize our anxiety about death determines whether we experience work as meaningful or meaningless. Unresolved death anxiety can result in heightened stress and even psychological burnout.

> *How we metabolize our anxiety about death determines whether we experience work as meaningful or meaningless.*

The logical way of dealing with these fears is through finding meaning. And finding purpose is part of this equation. For many—as part of the meaning equation—the meaning of life might be about leaving a legacy. They like to have some kind of impact. Here, the choices can be endless. But whatever actions people take, unless we've lived through their realities, we have no right to judge or condemn someone for their life choices. Similarly, we can't let others dictate how we live our lives because they haven't lived through what we've been or are currently going through. Other people should not write the script of our life. We must be something to do something. We need to remember that all serious daring starts from within.

> *Other people should not write the script of our life. We must be something to do something. We need to remember that all serious daring starts from within.*

Whatever our outlook, we have a responsibility in the world we live in. Life is not a spectator sport. If possible, we should try to make it a better place. After all, the one thing all humans share is that we all inhabit the same limited amount of real estate, which is Planet Earth. Isn't it up to us to make the best of it? Shouldn't we try to impact others in a positive way, to help others have a good life? In fact, if we want to help ourselves, we would be wise to try to help others. In the larger scheme of things, what's really worth doing is what we do for others. Also, it may make us feel better. In that respect, compassion is not merely a luxury. Without it, what would happen to the human species? To quote Albert Schweitzer, "Only such thinking as establishes the sway of the mental attitude of reverence for life can bring to mankind perpetual peace."[2]

> *To create a full life, it is essential to create meaning. With nothing meaningful in life, nothing will be interesting.*

Therefore, to create a full life, it is essential to create meaning. With nothing meaningful in life, nothing will be interesting. Sometimes, however, when things seem to be falling apart, we may not realize that they may actually be falling into place. Eventually, we should be able to look back at our life, saying "What an incredible story. What a great story all these years have been." The American essayist Ralph Waldo Emerson seemed to have been onto something when he said, "All life is an experiment. The more experiments you make the better."[3] When all is said and done, life can be a great adventure. We need to live life, not just exist. We may come to realize that the only impossible journey is the one we never went on. In other words, nothing ventured, nothing gained. If our life is going to have any meaning, we have to live it ourselves. We have to own it. We should remember that it is the fear of death that follows the fear of life. After all, it is the awareness of

---

[2] Albert Schweitzer (1949/1923). *The Civilization of Ethics*. Trans. C.T. Campion. London: Adam & Charles Black.
[3] Ralph Waldo Emerson (1911/1842). *The Journals of Ralph Waldo Emerson. Vol VI: 1841–1844*. Edited by Edward Waldo Emerson and Waldo Emerson Forbes. Boston, MA and New York: Houghton Mifflin Company, entry 11 November 1842.

our mortality that can lead us to wake up and live an authentic, meaningful life.

> *When all is said and done, life can be a great adventure. We need to live life, not just exist. We may come to realize that the only impossible journey is the one we never went on.*

16

The Authentizotic Puzzle

Be not afraid of life. Believe that life is worth living, and your belief will help create the fact.
—William James

There can be no peace without but through peace within.
—William Ellery Channing

I begin to see that a man's got to be in his own heaven to be happy.
—Mark Twain

Travelling

A new disciple in a monastery asked his widely travelled Zen master, "You have been to many places in the world. Which is the best place in the summer? Which is the best place during monsoon? Which is the best place to go during the winter?" As he was talking, it suddenly started pouring and the disciple quickly got out an umbrella. The master kept walking in the rain and said, "If you really want to be in the best place, you must go to the place where there is no summer, rain or winter!"

The new disciple then asked the Zen master, "Have you been there?" The Zen master responded affirmatively, and the disciple pressed him to say where it was.

"You find out and go!" said the Zen master and walked on without breaking his stride.

Best Place to Work

Since 1998, *Fortune* magazine has published an annual ranking of the "most admired US companies" based on criteria such as corporate values, innovation, financial growth, leadership effectiveness, maximizing human potential, and trust. An in-depth content analysis of the companies that rank highly in this list reveals that they are steeped in a number of values that are then also translated into specific forms of behavior—values such as trust, fun, candor, empowerment, respect for the individual, fairness, teamwork, entrepreneurship/innovation, customer orientation, accountability, continuous learning, and openness to change.

Although these values, and the practices associated with them, go a long way toward explaining the success of many of *Fortune*'s vibrant organizations, they alone cannot bring about exceptional performance. Additional conditions are necessary for getting the best out of people. In fact, organizations that excel across all these domains are what we have called "authentizotic"—a term derived from Greek *authenteekos* and *zoteekos*. These are the kinds of organizations that will set the standard in our present day-and-age. The authentizotic organization stands for something to strive for—an idealistic role model.

Authentizotic organizations are those that ask themselves: What can leaders do to make the lives of those in their organizations more meaningful? In this age of discontinuity, what can be done to minimize the negative side effects of work? What can be done to imbue employees with the kind of meaning that helps them feel fulfilled?

Authenteekos—"staying true to one's values"—is manifested within an organization by behaviors and practices that are aligned with the company's stated vision, mission, and values. It conveys the idea that the organization is authentic. In its broadest sense, the word "authentic" describes something that conforms to fact and is therefore worthy of trust and reliance. As a workplace label, authenticity implies that the organization has a compelling connective quality for its employees. This means that the organization's leader has communicated clearly and convincingly not only the how but also the why of every job, investing meaning in each person's tasks.

> *As a workplace label, authenticity implies that the organization has a compelling connective quality for its employees.*

On its part, *zoteekos*—"being vital to life"—implies that people are invigorated by their workplace and experience a sense of balance, well-being, and fulfillment. People in organizations to which the zoteekos label can be applied feel a sense of balance and completeness. In such organizations, the human need for exploration, closely associated with cognition and learning, is met. The zoteekos element of this type of organization allows for self-assertion in the workplace and produces a sense of effectiveness and competency, of autonomy, initiative, creativity, entrepreneurship, and industry.

In the century we're living in, organizational leaders will be challenged to design corporations that possess these authentizotic qualities. Working in these kinds of organizations will reduce organizational stress, provide a healthier existence, increase the imagination, and contribute to a more fulfilling life. Because authentizotic organizations help their employees maintain an effective balance between personal and organizational life, these are the organizations we need to hope and strive for. It is their concern for mental health that makes authentizotic organizations such optimistic places to work. As is stated very appropriately in an Arab proverb, "He who has health has hope, and he who has hope has everything!"

Moreover, leaders of authentizotic organizations noticeably infuse their organizations with meaning. They effectively articulate what they want to accomplish through communicating a vision of what the organization stands for, highlighting its fundamental *raison d'être*, and recognizing each employee's contribution to its success. Subscribing to the credo "profit with purpose," they create a balance between "what's good for the organization" and "what's good for the people who work there." Clearly, the authentizotic mindset relies on creating a culture of trust, mutual support, recognition, and engagement that unites people around a common vision. This fosters a people-centric culture where employees engage in meaningful work and give their best to the organization.

As can be imagined, the "best places to work" will have lower employee turnover than their competitors, recruit the best people, provide top-quality customer service, and create innovative products and services, all of which contribute to their overall financial success. Furthermore, such organizations provide higher job satisfaction and employee engagement. In short, people who are happy at work are more committed to the job.

> *People who are happy at work are more committed to the job.*

Although the authentizotic organization may be seen as a kind of utopia, or "ideal" state, it is always something to strive for. With this observation in mind, there are a number of underlying features that distinguish authentizotic organizations above all others:

- *They have a compelling mission* that everyone understands and signs up to. A values-based mission statement makes employees feel like they're part of something bigger, beyond the daily routine. Each person understands the role he or she plays in achieving that mission. As the saying goes, "people work for money but die for a cause." Thus, the organization's fundamental purpose goes beyond simply profit maximization; employees believe that they are creating products or services, or serving a cause, that add value to society. They feel good about the purpose and impact of their work. They not only stick around longer but enjoy a higher degree of job satisfaction and are more engaged. Such companies are more likely to be responsible contributors to their community and to the world at large. They recognize that, for reasons of sustainability, they must be responsive to all stakeholders.
- *The organization's culture and practices are aligned with the values they espouse.* These values are embraced at all levels; they are part of the organization's DNA. Unlike companies who merely pay lip service to what they say are their core values (but turn out to be nothing more than an exercise in public relations), in authentizotic organizations, employees who do not live the values are asked to shape up or leave.
- *Employees trust the people they work with and for.* The culture of trust goes both ways: employees implicitly trust their leaders to make the right decisions, while leaders trust employees to put the organization's needs first as they interact with various stakeholders. People are treated with respect and dignity. It makes for a safe environment. The culture of trust is also reflected in the way its leadership communicates the problems as well as the successes.
- *Leadership is not a solo act but a team sport.* These organizations are the opposite of the Darwinian "survival of the fittest" where everyone is out for themselves. Instead, people help and support each other. They are team-oriented, and, while politics are inevitable in any organization, these political dynamics are minimal in authentizotic ones. Internal competition and individualistic thinking are sidelined in favor of collaboration, thereby creating an enriching place to work.
- *The work environment emphasizes high-quality day-to-day relationships.* Employees enjoy working together and have fun. From a mental health

perspective, it is obvious that if people get along with, like, and respect those they work with, they derive a sense of belonging. Not surprisingly, working with people who are supportive and understanding fosters deeper personal connections and professional growth.
- *Fair process—the perception of a level playing-field for all.* As might be expected, fair pay and benefits are fundamental components of this, but equally important is the feeling that the leadership cares and is interested in employees' well-being. In authentizotic organizations, lay-offs are a last resort. Being treated fairly is a great motivator, exceeding anything that monetary rewards can procure.

> *Being treated fairly is a great motivator, exceeding anything that monetary rewards can procure.*

- *People feel that they are listened to.* Employees feel that they have a voice, that their input is valued. The leadership creates a culture that is participatory—where people can speak their mind and criticize without fear of reprisals. They actively listen to their employees' views and implement useful suggestions. Senior executives who trust the people who work for them push decision-making power downward to their subordinates. They give them as much autonomy as possible to choose when they work, where they work, and how best to get their work done. They recognize the difference between working hard and working smart. Moreover, they create places to work where entrepreneurial endeavors are encouraged.
- *A culture of recognition.* Efforts never go unappreciated and praise flows generously. Too often in organizations, appreciation is hard won, and attention is only given when an assignment goes wrong. Conversely, recognizing employees for their personal or team achievements creates a more meaningful experience. When people feel appreciated, the result is higher levels of engagement and employee retention.

> *Too often in organizations, appreciation is hard won, and attention is only given when an assignment goes wrong. Recognizing employees for their personal or team achievements creates a more meaningful experience.*

- *Ongoing opportunities and incentives to develop and grow.* Leaders recognize that people inherently want to be challenged and acquire new skills and go out of their way to provide opportunities to accelerate their personal growth. Furthermore, management makes a concerted effort to figure out ways to unlock each employee's potential, in the knowledge that it will benefit both the individual and the organization. While acknowledging that not all careers are built the same, management provides effective leadership development programs, resources for education outside of work, and platforms for coaching and mentoring.
- *Leaders really make a difference.* Top management walks the talk—they embrace and exemplify its values and goals, setting the direction in a way that can be described as true north. They ensure that everyone in the organization is treated with respect and care. They encourage senior executives to recognize the people who they supervise for the positive contributions that they make.
- *Information is shared.* Leadership ensures that communication and transparency are engendered at every level; they never stop thinking of how they can improve the communication flow upward, downward, and laterally. Putting transparent information systems in place helps employees to make more informed decisions.
- *Leadership realizes that people have a life outside of work.* Taking a holistic, long-term perspective, they acknowledge the importance of work/life balance. They go to great lengths to avoid employee burnout. They recognize that commitment is a give-and-take, not give or take. Again, this positively impacts organizational loyalty and commitment, making for a sustainable psychological contract between employer and employee.

Utopian or not, every organization would do well to strive for the qualities that characterize these best places to work. Those that tick every single box are rare, but at their core authentizotic organizations are distinguished by the high level of trust people have in their leaders, of pride and passion for their jobs, of enjoyment working with their colleagues, and the sense of meaning derived from the organization and its core values.

The Authentizotic Organization Checklist

The following checklist may provide a modicum of insight into whether your own organization is authentizotic. To figure out if that's the case, try to answer each question with *Yes* or *No*.

- Do you subscribe to the core values and mission of your organization?
- Does your work provide you with a strong sense of meaning?
- Do you enjoy working with the people in your organization?
- Does your organization manage to get the best out of you?
- Do the people in your organization live the values?
- Is trust a key element of your organization's culture?
- Do you believe that you are treated fairly in your organization?
- Does your organization have a team-oriented culture?
- Do you feel that you have a "voice" in your organization; that you are being listened to?
- Is it common in your organization to celebrate success and work well done?
- Is open communication a key characteristic of your organization?
- Is constructive feedback and coaching an ongoing process?
- Does your organization have a commitment to learning and development?
- Does your organization encourage entrepreneurial abilities and provide the resources to be creative?
- Do you have confidence in your organization's leadership?

The more often you answer "Yes," the more your organization has authentizotic qualities. If the majority of your answers are "No," your work environment may be draining rather than infusing you with energy.

> *To win in the marketplace, you first have to win in the workplace.*

Staying Out of the Wormhole

While working for an authentizotic organization will be desirable, very few organizations possess all the qualities needed to qualify as a "best place to work." As we have learned from experience, in too many organizations the culture can be dysfunctional, people work in ineffective ways, morale and motivation is low, and teams operate below par. Why this happens may ultimately come down to human nature: our ability to trust one another only so far, but perhaps not far enough; our self-centeredness and inability to see beyond our own needs. As has been said many times over: to win in the marketplace, you first have to win in the workplace. The main ingredient that makes for an authentizotic organization is trust. When trust is part of the organizational culture, people are more confident and more productive. They feel safe. Hence, the organization becomes a vibrant, networked web, connecting people up and down the hierarchy. And if there is such a thing as a magic recipe for trust, it may simply be that each individual treats other people as they would like to be treated. To subscribe to the Golden Rule, "do unto others as you would have them do unto you," will always be good advice. Otherwise, who knows, what goes around, may come around!

17

Love and Work

Love and work are the cornerstones of our humanness.
—Sigmund Freud

The strongest guard is placed at the gateway to nothing … Maybe because the condition of emptiness is too shameful to be divulged.
—F. Scott Fitzgerald

I felt as if I was the only person awake in a city of sleepwalkers. That's an illusion, of course. When you walk through a crowd of strangers it's next door to impossible not to imagine that they're all waxworks, but probably they're thinking just the same about you.
—George Orwell

Yes

A person went to a retreat for a period of silence. After he had finished, he felt much better, calmer, and stronger. Still, something was missing. He expressed his concerns to the person in charge of the retreat and was told to talk to a wise woman before leaving, who happened to be in residence.

Having thought about the matter for a while, on meeting the woman he asked her, "How do you find peace?"

The wise woman said: "I say yes. I make it a point to say yes to everything that happens."

When the man returned home, he felt enlightened. Clearly, there is something to be said for having a positive attitude. It makes everyone feel better.

The "Healthy" Individual

In our day-and-age, we perceive many themes in the world of work that are disquieting. Among the most dominant of those themes is stress and burnout in the workplace. Statistics that measure stress—for example, tallies of illness, underperformance, and absenteeism—tell a dramatic tale of dysfunctionality at work. In many organizations the balance between working life and private life has been completely lost. Organizational horror stories abound—stories about dysfunctional leadership, work overload, conflicting job demands, poor communication, lack of opportunities for career advancement, inequities in performance evaluations and pay, restrictions on behavior, and excessive travel (and the connection between these problems and depressive reactions, alcoholism, drug abuse, and sleep disorders).

Yet, work doesn't need to be a stress carrier. On the contrary, in our role as organizational clinicians we have found out that work can be an anchor of psychological well-being, a means of establishing identity and maintaining self-esteem. Sigmund Freud's dictum that mental health consists of "*lieben und arbeiten*" (loving and working) still retains a ring of truth.[1] In that respect, organizations are invested with a considerable amount of psychological meaning by those who daily cross their threshold. Accomplishing something tangible and positive through work can give workers a point of stability in a highly unstable world (just as frustrating, dissatisfying work can exacerbate instability, contributing to excessive stress and burnout). In fact, organizations are ideal outlets to help their participants cope with the stresses and strains of daily life.

> *Work can be an anchor of psychological well-being, a means of establishing identity and maintaining self-esteem.*

Given the importance of individual psychological well-being for organizational functioning, an item that should be high on everybody's agenda (as mentioned in Chapter 16) is creating workplaces that are healthy—i.e., those that help people feel good about themselves and their endeavors, and that contribute to (and reinforce) adaptive functioning.

However, the basis of what it is that makes organizations vibrant—makes them great places to work—begins with an understanding of the well-functioning individual. To gain that understanding, we must ask, under what

---

[1] From correspondence with Alfred Adler.

conditions does a person feel most alive? And what can those who are in charge of an organization do to make this happen?

Responding to this question is easier said than done. Definitions of what makes for a "healthy" individual seem to vary depending on the person making the observations. But when psychotherapists or coaches are asked what makes for a well-functioning person, they generally say that "healthy" people are those individuals who operate at their full mental capacity. These helping professionals see their role as encouraging their clients to gain insights into their goals and motivations, helping them better understand their strengths and weaknesses, and preventing them from engaging in self-destructive activities. The emphasis is on widening people's area of choice, thereby enabling them to choose freely rather than be led by forces outside of their awareness.

> *A well-functioning, "healthier" person is one who operates at their full mental capacity.*

Although this answer has merit, we suggest that it needs some elaboration. From our experience in working with large numbers of executives, we propose that healthier people possess a common set of characteristics. (We say healthier rather than healthy because health and illness will be dimensions on a continuum.) The most salient of these characteristics are described below:

- Healthier people possess a stable sense of identity; that is, they have a good sense of who they are.
- They have a great capacity for reality testing.
- They resort to mature defense mechanisms and take responsibility for their actions, refusing to blame others for setbacks.
- They have a strong sense of self-efficacy, believing in their own ability to control the events that affect their lives; and they are resourceful.
- They have a healthy perception of their abilities, including their body and its functioning; therefore, they do not engage in self-destructive activities due to cognitive distortions.
- They experience the full range of affects; they do not suffer from alexithymia or color-blindness with respect to their emotions. They live intensely and are passionate about what they do, finding sexuality fulfilling.
- They know how to manage anxiety, and they do not easily lose control or resort to impulsive acts.

- They have the capacity to establish and cultivate relationships. They actively maintain a support network, and they know how to use help and advice.
- They have a sense of belonging and connectedness, viewing themselves as part of a larger group. They obtain a great sense of satisfaction about the social context in which they are living.
- They know how to deal with issues of dependency and separation. Having gone through the process of individuation in a constructive manner during their younger years, they do not suffer from developmental arrest. They possess a secure sense of attachment. As people in their own right, they do not resort to clinging or avoidant behavior. On the contrary, they are able to establish mature relationships.
- They are mentally strong enough to deal with the setbacks and disappointments that are an inevitable part of the trajectory of life. They know how to handle depressive feelings and have a great capacity to work through loss.
- They know how to handle ambivalent feelings. Consequently, they are able to see people in a balanced manner.
- They are creative and possess a sense of playfulness, having the capacity to non-conform.
- They have a positive outlook toward the world. They can reframe experiences in a constructive way. They are always able to fantasize about a more positive picture of the future. Whatever setbacks may come their way, they tend to retain a great sense of positivity.
- They have the capacity for self-observation and self-analysis and are highly motivated to spend time on self-reflection.

Motivational Need Systems

Describing behavior is a necessary but insufficient condition for understanding why people do what they do. The above descriptions of the characteristics of "healthier" individuals remain incomplete unless we also pay attention to the underlying forces that place an individual on the healthy-to-dysfunctional continuum. Because a healthy outlook toward life is the outcome of a lengthy process of development, we must also look to each individual's "inner theater."

> *The core of an individual's inner theater is shaped around the motivational need systems on which the choices one makes are grounded.*

The core of an individual's inner theater is shaped around the motivational need systems on which the choices one makes are grounded. These need systems become operational in infancy and continue throughout the life cycle, altered by the forces of age, learning, and maturation. Motivational need systems are the driving forces that make people behave the way they do. Developmental "resolutions"—self-stabilizing responses to emotional reactions based on motivational needs—determine the content of the inner script of an individual, enabling the formation of values, beliefs, and attitudes.

Clearly, some of the motivational need systems that drive people center around low-level, primary human needs: the most fundamental motivational system regulates a person's physiological requirements, for example (dealing with factors such as hunger, thirst, sleep, and breathing); another system encompasses an individual's needs for sensual enjoyment and later sexual excitement; a third system develops in response to the need to respond aversively to certain situations through antagonism and withdrawal. Other systems operate at a higher level, dealing with needs for attachment/affiliation and exploration/assertion. Although all motivational systems impact the work situation, it is these higher-level systems that are of particular interest for life in organizations.

Among humans there exists an innately unfolding experience of human relatedness. Humankind's essential humanness is found in the seeking of relationships with other people, of being part of something. The need for belonging concerns the process of engagement with another human being, the universal experience of wanting to be close to others. It also relates to the pleasure of sharing and affirmation. When this need for intimate engagement is extrapolated to groups, the desire to enjoy intimacy can be described as a need for affiliation. Both attachment and affiliation serve an emotional balancing role by confirming the individual's self-worth and contributing to his or her sense of self-esteem.

> *Among humans there exists an innately unfolding experience of human relatedness. Humankind's essential humanness is found in the seeking of relationships with other people, of being part of something.*

The other need that is central to this discussion—the need for exploration—involves the ability to play and to work. This need also begins early in life. Child observation has shown that novelty and the discovery of the effects of certain actions cause prolonged states of attentive arousal in infants. Similar reactions to opportunities for exploration continue into adulthood. Closely tied to this need for exploration is self-assertion—the ability to choose what one likes to do. Exploratory-assertive motivation produces a sense of effectiveness and competency; playful exploration and manipulation of the environment in response to exploratory-assertive motivation produces a sense of mastery, autonomy, initiative, and industry. Because striving, competing, and seeking mastery are fundamental motivational forces of the human personality, exercising assertiveness—following our preferences, acting in a determined manner—serves as a form of self-affirmation. This striving continues into adulthood.

> *Need systems create a subjective reality that guides each of us through life, shaping our outlook on the world ... . To be healthy, that subjective reality needs to be congruent with objective reality; that is, how we perceive ourselves and our surroundings needs to reflect external reality accurately.*

What we are trying to point out is that, at a very basic level, the scripts in our inner theater are determined by our responses to the various motivational need systems. In other words, those need systems create a subjective reality that guides each of us through life, shaping our outlook on the world. In order for individuals to be healthy, that subjective reality needs to be congruent with objective reality; that is, how we perceive ourselves and our surroundings needs to reflect external reality accurately. This "match" between subjective and social worlds creates a sense of authenticity and constancy in the individual. Thus, organizations hoping to foster an environment in which people feel really alive must keep this sort of congruence in mind.

In our search for continuity in a world of discontinuity, the striving for congruence between inner and outer reality offers a way to challenge the humdrum of day-to-day life. It will always be an important part of the agenda of change agents using the psychodynamic-systemic methodology. By following this agenda, implicitly or explicitly, we hope to help our clients find meaning in whatever they're doing, affirming a sense of authenticity, fostering a sense of accomplishment and personal competence, and creating a higher-level motivation that drives them to transcend their traditional activities. Work is an integral part of our clients' search for meaning; it can contribute to a sense of significance and orientation, offer a way to transcend personal concerns, and create a sense of continuity and order. Leaving a legacy through work is an affirmation of our clients' sense of self and identity.

> *In our search for continuity in a world of discontinuity, the striving for congruence between inner and outer reality offers a way to challenge the humdrum of day-to-day life.*

Given the importance of these basic human motivational needs, we also emphasize to our clients that organizational leadership has a responsibility to create the circumstances that allow people to do tasks in the workplace that are experienced as consequential. Subjective experiences and actions need to be made meaningful. This means that individuals should be able to work in ways that make sense to them, leading to a congruence between personal and collective objectives. Facilitating congruence between the inner and outer worlds of employees in this way will contribute to individual and organizational health.

> *Organizational leadership has a responsibility to create the circumstances that allow people to do tasks in the workplace that are experienced as consequential.*

In light of our earlier discussion, the readers of this book should not be surprised to learn that leaders who want to get the best out of their people—who want to create an ambiance in which their people feel inspired and choose to give their best—must pay attention to the exploration/assertion and attachment/affiliation motivational need systems. To that end, they have to engage in a number of activities that help to ensure congruence between the inner and outer realities of their workers/employees.

To address people's exploration/assertion motivational need system, we also stress that the people who lead an organization must create the conditions that foster a sense of competence. It implies that learning and personal development should be an essential part of a well-functioning organization's DNA. To prevent stagnation, continuous learning will be essential. On-the-job growth and development offer a strategy for reaffirming the self and preserving personal equilibrium. When the exploration/assertion motivational need system is blocked, however, frustration increases, and creative action dissipates.

With these need systems in mind, we encourage the leaders of organizations to create a greater sense of self-determination among their people. For the sake of organizational mental health, we emphasize that it is essential that the people who work in their organizations have a feeling of control over their lives. Conditions should be created whereby they see themselves not as mere peons in the larger scheme of things but as capable masters of their own existence.

At the same time, leadership must imbue each of the people who work for them with the conviction that their work can have impact, that his or her actions make a difference and contribute meaningfully to organizational performance. Believing that each member of the organization has a voice is what empowerment is all about.

> *Meaning refers to the extent to which one experiences life as being directed and motivated by valued goals—i.e. that whatever we are doing matters. We can even see meaning as an experiential byproduct of a life lived in the way it should be lived.*

Finding Meaning in Life

Meaning and motivation play a central role in an individual's sense of self-fulfillment. Consequently, in trying to understand themselves better, we help our clients (as already touched upon in Chapter 16) to create a compelling self-narrative centered around meaning. Here, meaning can be redefined as *intent*, or *significance*. It refers to the extent to which one experiences life as being directed and motivated by valued goals—in other words, that whatever we are doing matters. We can even see meaning as an experiential byproduct of a life lived in the way it should be lived. At the same time, however, meaning has deeper layers that need to be explored if we are to find what's truly important to us.

> *Meaning is the symbolic value of something, whereas purpose is a goal. ... To mean something is to have value and significance. To have a purpose implies to bring value to something, to make something significant.*

Yet, in popular use meaning and purpose tend to be used interchangeably—and often rightly so, when we refer to the worth or value of something. For example, the meaning or purpose of life could refer to the worth or significance of life: "my purpose would be to create something meaningful." This interchangeability is not a given, however. For instance, the comment, "there is no meaning in my life" is not the same as "there is no purpose in my life." That's because meaning is the symbolic value of something, whereas purpose is a goal. Thus, to mean something is *to have value and significance*. To have a purpose, however, implies *to bring value* to something, *to make something significant*. In other words, purpose can guide life decisions, influence behavior, shape goals, offer a sense of direction, *as well as* create meaning. It has a future connotation. In contrast, meaning is the end of purpose. It refers to the past, the present, and the future. Of course, without a sense of purpose, it is hard to find meaning. Also, at times, whatever our purpose is, it may have no meaning at all. We may be engaged in pointless, hollow activities.

> *Without a sense of purpose, it is hard to find meaning. Also, at times, whatever our purpose is, it may have no meaning at all. We may be engaged in pointless, hollow activities.*

Basically, we point out to our clients that there are five pillars that influence the way that we experience meaning: **belonging**, **purpose**, **competence**, **control**, and **transcendence**. These pillars are defined as follows:

Belonging: Being hardwired to build connections—as social creatures—we have the sense that our presence and/or absence means something to other people. We experience the sense of being part of a community.

Purpose: A future-oriented construct in the form of a goal, target, or objective to be reached. It implies doing something valuable, engaging in something significant. This sense of purpose will guide our life decisions, influence our behavior, shape our goals, and offer a sense of direction.

Competence: A feeling that we are moving forward, progressing, honing our skills. It is doing what we really love to do. It concerns taking pride in what we are accomplishing.

Control: A sense that our life, our decisions, and our actions are very much determined by matters we believe are under our control. It pertains to the feeling of owning our own life.

Transcendence: A feeling of unity and communion with something much bigger than us. It pertains to what contribution our clients can make to society, how to engage in various forms of self-improvement with the purpose of being helpful to others.

> *It is our search for meaning that makes us truly human.*

It is our search for meaning that makes us (*Homo sapiens*) truly human. Clearly, consciousness—the awareness of our inner and outer reality—is unique to humanity. It compels us to search for meaning. It will be meaning that makes us live. It will be meaning that incites us to go beyond our immediate "here and now" urges and demands. It compels us to figure out who we are, what's important to us. It helps us understand how our external world affects our outlook on life, and how the scripts in our inner theater affect why we do what we do, and that we will be living according to our beliefs and values. (A summary of these five pillars that make up meaning can be found in Fig. 17.1).

Meaning in Life Questionnaire

To help our clients assess how effectively they deal with these five important dimensions in life, we have used the *Meaning in Life Questionnaire* (see Fig. 17.2, p. 182). It is meant to offer a quick assessment of which of the five pillars coaching clients may need to work on.

We challenge our clients to weave these responses into a compelling personal narrative. Using the outcome of the questionnaire as a basis, when appropriate, we suggest our clients should be able to tell a story that explains the role of these five pillars in their life's journey. The stories they tell, and the way they tell them, reveal who they are and become an essential part of themselves. Taking the disparate pieces of their life and putting them together into a coherent narrative allows them to understand their life as a whole. The ability to tell their story will help them to enact whatever they are doing. In fact, their personal stories will give them a sense of direction and a purpose

Our Existential Challenges

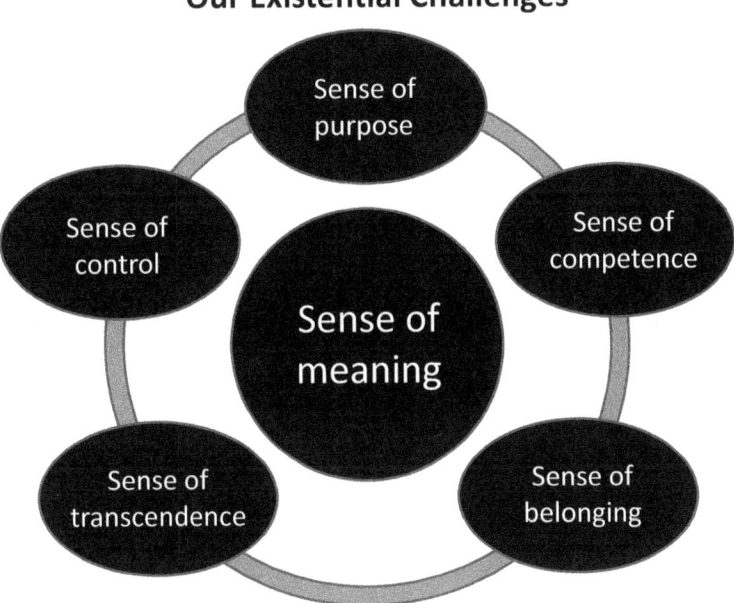

Fig. 17.1 Our existential challenges

and help them to recognize whether they have adopted a satisfactory balance between work and the rest of their life. Their challenge is to manage the pressures placed on them by their organizations and manage their internal pressures to have a satisfactory life. And as their personal narrative creates a story worth telling, it may also help them to arrive at something bigger than themselves.

Developing Reflective People

The challenge is to make our clients more reflective leaders—people who do not just do things but who also have the capacity to reflect and listen. As Epictetus said, "We have two ears and one mouth so that we can listen twice as much as we speak."[2] In a coaching setting, in every conversation the coach and the person being coached need to ask themselves a series of questions, the most important of which are: "How do I feel listening to this person?" and "What effect does this person have on me?"

---

[2] Epictetus (1909/c. 50–135 AD). "Fragments of Epictetus." In *Noble Thoughts of Epictetus*. Selected and edited by Dana Estes. Boston, MA: Dana Estes & Company, no. 112, page 84.

Meaning in Life Questionnaire

p__ I am leading a very purposeful life.

c__ My life is full of interesting learning experiences.

b__ My interactions with other people give me a lot of pleasure.

co__ It is up to me to make something of my life.

p__ I look forward to the new, exciting challenges that each day come my way.

c__ I very much enjoy what I am doing.

co__ I feel free to make whatever life choices I want.

b__ I have a very fulfilling social network.

t__ When I die, I believe that I have led a very worthwhile life.

c__ I can completely lose myself in whatever I do.

b__ I am very close to my family and friends.

co__ I feel very much in control of my life.

p__ I have always been very effective in pursuing my life's goals.

t__ I get a lot of pleasure out of helping others.

t__ I am actively involved in dealing with issues that are larger than me.

> 7—strongly agree
> 6—agree
> 5—slightly agree
> 4—neither agree or disagree
> 3—slightly disagree
> 2—disagree
> 1—strongly disagree

Scoring

Add up your responses. The range of scores is from 15 (lowest possible) to 105 (highest possible). A high score suggests that you have many psychological resources and strengths. (Key: b=belonging; p=purpose; c=competence; co=control; t=transcendence).

Fig. 17.2 Meaning in Life Questionnaire

> *Coaches are cognizant of the fact that many people live under the illusion that they understand what is being said to them.*

Leadership coaches are cognizant of the fact that many people live under the illusion that they understand what is being said to them. This is not the same thing, however, as being sure that what one hears is what the speaker means. Many attempts at communication are nullified by our tendency to say too much. Most people do not learn while they are talking. There is an old Chinese saying that tells us, "To listen well is as powerful a means of influence as to talk well and is as essential to all true conversation."

With the clinical approach, we support the development of reflective practitioners by trying to use our own unconscious as a receptive organ for the unconscious signals the other person is transmitting. We always look out for transferential and countertransferential reactions—i.e., how responses based on earlier relationships color the discourse we are engaged in. At all times, clients are encouraged to appreciate that behavior that may have been effective at one stage in their life has become obsolete, and that it would be better to avoid playing a role that is no longer appropriate.

Following the notion of creating reflective practitioners, we also warn our clients to be wary whenever they feel a strong urge to move into action. The "action trap" can be exactly that, leading them to take some kind of action that they may regret later. Perhaps the best time to hold their tongue is when they feel they must say something or have an explosive reaction. All too often, acting is a substitute for thinking—a refusal to reflect on why they are doing what they are doing.

> *Be wary whenever you feel a strong urge to move into action. All too often, acting is a substitute for thinking.*

The world is full of people who have stopped listening to themselves. Some listen only to others to learn what they ought to do, how they ought to behave, and what values and beliefs they ought to be living for. But if we do not believe in "us" until someone else reveals we have something valuable, worth listening to, worthy of our trust, or sacred to our touch, we lose part of ourselves. And this is where an executive coach can help.

> *If we do not believe in "us" until someone else reveals we have something valuable, worth listening to, worthy of our trust, or sacred to our touch, we lose part of ourselves.*

Once we help people believe in themselves, they can risk curiosity, wonder, spontaneous delight, or any experience that reveals the human spirit. Although other people's ideas will have merit, executives have to practice how to listen to their own inner voice. If executives acquire this ability, they will have a clearer idea of themselves and be better at recognizing what is important to them.

Based on the clinical paradigm, with its recognition of the importance of unconscious processes, the more psychodynamic-systemic approach creates for our clients a greater self-awareness. It helps them to become aware not only of their conscious thoughts, but also of their unconscious prejudices, biases, and habits. As one recent participant of our group coaching workshops reported: "This intervention method [teaches] you things about yourself that will help you influence others by better understanding them first." Or to quote the Roman emperor Marcus Aurelius, an exemplary reflective leader: "Dig inside yourself. Inside there is a spring of goodness ready to gush at any moment, if you keep digging."[3]

Making the Best of a Poor Hand of Cards

The aim of most forms of personal growth and development is the achievement of self-direction and autonomy. Paradoxically, total autonomy leads to chaos; total control leads to suffocation. Wisdom implies realizing that we cannot have it both ways: being impulsive and being conformist. Our challenge becomes feeling free in a gentle harness, meaning that we are willing to subordinate our impulsive strivings to controls from the outside that evolve into self-control. From the start our challenge is to create a wider area of choice. That is what mental health is all about.

> *Total autonomy leads to chaos; total control leads to suffocation. Wisdom implies realizing that we cannot have it both ways: being impulsive and being conformist.*

---

[3] Marcus Aurelius (2014/161–180 CE). *Meditations*. Trans. Martin Hammond. Harmondsworth, UK: Penguin, book 7, meditation 59.

The journey taken during our interventions is to educate for optimal personal freedom, while considering the demands of reality and society. Our challenge is to modify people's inner script. And we have to make it *our* script, not a script that is written by others. We need to recognize and own our own impulses and actions. We have to own our own lives.

During our interventions, clients learn that in order to develop a strong sense of what they are all about, to achieve growth and maturation, it is first necessary to be able to trust others. Trust will fuel self-disclosure and learning. These trusted others will be the guides on their inner journey. Helped by the others, the participants will gain a better perspective on their past, their present, their future, their wishes and desires. The participants also discover newer patterns of behavior more suited for present-day reality. Perspective springs from seeing things in context. The participants acquire greater control over their actions so that new situations can be approached more flexibly. They will be helped to overcome self-defeating patterns of behaviors and thoughts. Consequently, a new, internalized dialogue will evolve that makes the person more resistant to internal and external stressors. And hopefully, a more flexible, self-directive, and mature way of dealing with others will be acquired. The result is progressively more freedom to modify conflictual attitudes and behavior in the direction of more adaptive and flexible responses to changing circumstances; the creation of realistic opportunities for satisfying interpersonal needs. Such interventions help clients realize that they have choices, so that rather than responding to a new relationship in the old manner they can stop, think, and choose other ways of doing this. And it will help them to create healthier organizations.

> *Perspective springs from seeing things in context.*

One of the lessons we have learned from listening to senior executives is that all outwards success, when it is truly appreciated, has to be matched by inward success. To succeed in whatever we are trying to do, we need faith and confidence in our own powers. We have to realize that living a full life is not just the luck of having been dealt a good hand of cards. On the contrary, it is the ability to make the best of a poor hand. And the recipe (if there exists such a thing) for living life to the fullest is to laugh more often, play, appreciate beautiful things, have deep friendships, take pleasure in our family, and enjoy whatever we are doing.

> *All outwards success, when it is truly appreciated, has to be matched by inward success.*

The journey that is life is what counts, not the destination. How we cope with the inevitable obstacles we will encounter will determine the richness of the journey. And as we will discover when we take this journey of self-exploration, most of the obstacles are human made. Most often, we are the ones who made them. If we want, we can change them. We can learn from experience.

> *We have to realize that living a full life is not just the luck of having been dealt a good hand of cards. On the contrary, it is the ability to make the best of a poor hand.*

Epigraph Sources

Chapter 1

Joseph Butler (1887/1726). 'Sermon VII: Upon the Character of Balaam.' In *Human Nature and Other Sermons*. London: Cassell.

Marcus Aurelius (1887/170–180 AD). *The Meditations of Marcus Aurelius*. Trans. Jeremy Collier; Introduction and Notes by Alice Zimmern. London: Walter Scott.

Miguel de Cervantes Saavedra (1896/1605–1615). *The Ingenious Gentleman Don Quixote of La Mancha*. Trans. John Ormsby. New York: Dodd, Mead and Company.

Chapter 2

Sophocles (1911/c. 429 BC). *Oedipus, King of Thebes*. Trans. Gilbert Murray. London: George Allen & Unwin.

Hippocrates (1849/400 BC). 'Epidemics Book I.' In *The Genuine Works of Hippocrates*. Trans. Francis Adams. London: Sydenham Society.

Marcel Proust (1927/1922). *Cities of the Plain*. Vol. 4 of *Remembrance of Things Past* [*Sodome et Gomorrhe I*]. Trans C.K. Scott Moncrief. London: Chatto & Windus.

Chapter 3

Jean de la Fontaine (1913/1678). 'The Horoscope.' In *The Original Fables of La Fontaine*. Trans. F.C. Tilney. London: J.M. Dent, Book VIII, No. 16.

William Jennings Bryan (1913/1899). '"America's Mission", a speech delivered by the leader of the Democratic Party at the Washington Day banquet given by the Virginia Democratic Association at Washington, DC (22 February 1899).' In *Speeches of William Jennings Bryan*, vol. 2. New York and London: Funk & Wagnalls.

Lewis Carroll (1898/1865). *Alice's Adventures in Wonderland*. London: The Macmillan Company.

Chapter 4

Marcus Aurelius (1910/170–180 AD). *Meditations of Marcus Aurelius*. Trans. George Long. London: Blackie & Son, Book VI, Meditation 21.

Henry Melvill (1855). 'Partaking in Other Men's Sins,' an address at St. Margaret's Church, Lothbury, England, 12 June 1855. In *Golden Lectures*, Vol. 3. London: James Paul, p. 454.

Isaac Newton (1675). Letter to Robert Hooke. Original can be seen at https://digitallibrary.hsp.org/index.php/Detail/objects/9792.

Chapter 5

Lao Tzu (1905/sixth century BC). 'Chapter LXXVI.' In *The Tao Teh King: A Short Study in Comparative Religion*. Trans. C. Spurgeon Medhurst. Chicago, IL: Theosophical Book Concern.

Hippocrates (1849/400 BC). 'Epidemics Book I.' In *The Genuine Works of Hippocrates*. Trans. Francis Adams. London: Sydenham Society.

Marcus Cicero (1926/March, 43 BC). *Philippics*. Translated by Walter C. A. Ker. Cambridge, MA: Harvard University Press, Philippic 12. II. 5.

Chapter 6

Proverb, published by Charles Spurgeon (1889). *The Salt-cellars: Being a Collection of Proverbs, Together with Homely Notes Thereon.* London: Passmore and Alabaster, p. 89.

Jalálu'ddín Rúmí (1926/c. 1258 ff). 'The King and the Handmaiden.' In *The Mathnawí of Jalálu'ddín Rúmí*. Trans. Reynold A. Nicholson. London: Cambridge University Press for the Trustees of the EJW Gibb Memorial, Book I.

Anon (1740). *The Life and Adventures of Mrs. Christian Davies.* London: R. Montagu.

Chapter 7

Archimedes in Heath, T.L. (1897). *The Works of Archimedes.* Cambridge: University Press, p. xix.

William James (1902). 'Lecture IX, "Conversion".' In *The Varieties of Religious Experience: A Study in Human Nature.* New York, London and Bombay: Longmans, Green, and Co.

Sydney Smith (1849). 'Lecture XIX: On the Conduct of the Understanding, Part II.' In *Elementary Sketches of Moral Philosophy.* London: Spottiswoodes and Shaw.

Chapter 8

Galileo Galilei (1623). *Il Saggiatore.* Roma: Appresso Giacomo Mascardi.

Charles de Secondat, Baron de Montesquieu (1730/1721). 'Letter LVII.' In *Lettres persanes* [*Persian Letters.*] Trans. J. Ozell. London: J. Tonson.

Marcus Tullius Cicero (1913/44 BC). *De Officiis* [*On Moral Duty*; *The Offices.*] Trans. W. Miller. Book 1, Chapter 4, §13. London: William Heinemann.

Chapter 9

Epiphanius Wilson (1900). 'The Analects of Confucius, Book XVII.' In *Chinese Literature*. New York and London: The Colonial Press.

Mahatma Gandhi (1913). 'General Knowledge About Health XXXII: Accidents Snake-Bite.' In *Indian Opinion* (Gujarati).

Woodrow Wilson (1918/1916, 10 July). 'Address to World's Salesmanship Congress, Detroit (10 July 1916).' In *President Wilson's State Papers and Addresses*. New York: George H. Doran Company.

Chapter 10

Charlotte Brontë (1853). *Villette*. London: Smith, Elder & Co., Chapter V. Published under the pseudonym Currer Bell.

Francis Herbert Bradley (1930). *Aphorisms*. Oxford: Clarendon Press, No. 8. Published posthumously.

Antoine de Saint-Exupéry (1943). *Le Petit Prince*. New York: Reynall & Hitchcock. In French and English. Author's translation.

Chapter 11

Elizabeth Cady Stanton (1895). *The Woman's Bible*. New York: The European Publishing Company, Part 1, Introduction.

Jalálu'ddín Rúmí (1925–1940/ c. 1258 ff). *The Mathnawí of Jalálu'ddín Rúmí*. Trans. Reynold A. Nicholson. London: Cambridge University Press for the Trustees of the EJW Gibb Memorial, Volumes V and VI.

Ovid (1893/c. 43 BC–c. 18 AD). From Ars Amatoria, Book I. In *Dictionary of Quotations*. Selected and Compiled by the Rev. James Wood. London: Frederick Warne & Co.

Chapter 12

Ralph Waldo Emerson (1909/1841). 'Self-Reliance.' In *Essays by Ralph Waldo Emerson*. Selected and edited by Edna H.L. Turpin. New York: Charles E. Merrill Co.

Fridtof Nansen (1927). *Adventure and Other Papers*. London: L. and Virginia Woolf, Hogarth Press.

Paul Valéry (1944). *Tel Quel*. Paris: Gallimard, LXXXIX. Author's translation.

Chapter 13

Gilbert Keith Chesterton (1894–1898). 'Comparisons.' In *The Notebook*. BL MS Add. 73334, fo. 5.

Johan Huizinga (1939/1935). *In de schaduwen van morgen*. Haarlem: H.D. Tjeenk Willink. Original: 'Willen wij cultuur behouden, dan moeten wij voortgaan met cultuur te scheppen.' Author's translation.

Friedrich Nietzsche (1923/1886). *Beyond Good and Evil*. Trans. Helen Zimmern. London: George Allen & Unwin, Aphorism 146.

Chapter 14

Mark Twain (1909). *Is Shakespeare Dead? From My Autobiography*. New York: Harper & Bros.

The two remaining epigraphs stand as a tribute to Sudhir Kakar, a close friend of Professor Kets de Vries.

Chapter 15

Epicurus (1926/341–270 BC). 'Fragment 68.' In *Epicurus*. Oxford: Clarendon Press.

Edgar Allen Poe (1875/1829). 'Alone.' In *Scribner's Monthly*, September 1875.

Jalálu'ddín Rúmí (1925–1940/1258–1273). *The Mathnawi of Jalalu'ddin Rumi*. Trans. Reynold A. Nicholson. London: Cambridge University Press.

Chapter 16

William James (1912/1897). 'Is Life Worth Living?' In *The Will to Believe and Other Essays in Popular Philosophy*. New York: Longmans, Green, and Co.

William Ellery Channing (1877/1839). 'Lecture on War.' In *The Works of William E. Channing*. Boston, MA: American Unitarian Association, pp. 664–679.

Mark Twain (1922/1916). *The Mysterious Stranger [and Other Stories]*. New York and London: Harper & Brothers. Published posthumously.

Chapter 17

Sigmund Freud from his correspondence with Alfred Adler (1899–1911).

F. Scott Fitzgerald (1933). *Tender is the Night*. New York: Charles Scribner's Sons.

George Orwell (1939). *Coming Up for Air*. London: Victor Gollancz.

Recommended Readings

To make this book more readable, we have not used references to support our various propositions. However, in case the reader is interested in pursuing the theoretical background of many of our suggestions of how to go about personal and organizational transformation, the following reading list may be helpful:

Balint, M. (1957). *The Doctor, His Patient and the Illness*. New York: International Universities Press.
Bandura, A. (1997). *Self-efficacy: The Exercise of Control*. New York: W. H. Freeman.
Basch, M. F. (1995). *Doing Brief Psychotherapy*. New York: Basic Books.
Bion, W. (1977). *Group Dynamics: A Review*. London: Routledge.
Bowlby, J. (1969). *Attachment and Loss*. New York: Basic Books.
Crits-Christoph, P. and Barber, J. P. (Eds). (1991). *Handbook of Short-term Dynamic Psychotherapy*. New York: Basic Books.
Davonloo, H. (Ed.). (1994). *Basic Principles and Techniques in Short-term Dynamic Psychotherapy*. London: Jason Aronson.
Erikson, E. H. (1963). *Childhood and Society*. New York: W. W. Norton & Society.
Flaherty, J. (2005). *Coaching: Evoking Excellence in Others*. Burlington, MA: Elsevier Butterworth-Heinemann.
Foulkes, S. H. (1975). *Group Analytic Psychotherapy: Methods and Principles*. London: Gordon & Breach.

Frankl, V. (1962). *Man's Search for Meaning: An Introduction to Logotherapy*. Boston, MA: Beacon Press.

Freud, S. (1933). New Introductory Lectures. *The Standard Edition of the Complete Psychological Works of Sigmund Freud*, J. Strachey (Ed.). London: The Hogarth Press and the Institute of Psychoanalysis.

Gabriel, Y. (1999). *Organizations in Depth*. London: Sage.

Goleman, D. (1995). *Emotional Intelligence*. London: Bloomsbury.

Goleman, D. (1998). *Working With Emotional Intelligence*. New York: Bantam Books.

Greenberg, J. R. and Mitchell, S. A. (1983). *Object Relations in Psychoanalytic Theory*. Cambridge, MA: Harvard University Press.

Greenson, R. R. (1967). *The Technique and Practice of Psychoanalysis*. New York: International University Press.

Groves, J. E. (Ed.). (1996). *Essential Papers on Short-term Dynamic Therapy*. New York: New York University Press.

Gustavson, J. P. (1986). *The Complex Secret of Brief Psychotherapy*. New York: Norton.

Hackman, J. R. (2002). *Leading Teams: Setting the Stage for Great Performances*. Boston, MA: Harvard Business School Press.

Heatherton, T. and Weinberger, J. L. (Eds). (1994). *Can Personality Change?* Washington, DC: American Psychological Association.

Heimann, P., Klein, M., and Money-Kyrle, R. (Eds). (1985). *New Directions in Psychoanalysis: The Significance of Infant Conflict in the Pattern of Adult Behavior*. London: Karnac.

Hirschhorn, L. (1988). *The Workplace Within: Psychodynamics of Organizational Life*. Cambridge, MA: The MIT Press.

Hogan, R. T., Johnson, J., et al. (Eds). (1997). *Handbook of Personality Psychology*. New York: Morgan Kaufman.

Horowitz, M. J., Marmor, C., et al. (1984). *Personality Styles and Brief Psychotherapy*. New York: Basic Books.

Hudson, F. M. (1999). *The Handbook of Coaching: A Comprehensive Resource Guide for Managers, Executives, Consultants, and Human Resource Professionals*. San Francisco, CA: Jossey-Bass.

Janis, I. L. (1982). *Groupthink: Psychological Studies of Policy Decisions and Fiascoes*. Boston, MA: Houghton Mifflin.

Jaques, E. (1955). Social systems as a defense against persecutory and depressive anxiety. In M. Klein, P. Heimann, & R. E. Money-Kyrle (Eds), *New Directions in Psychoanalysis*. London: Tavistock.

Kegan, R. and Laskow Lahey, L. (2009). *Immunity to Change*. Boston, MA: Harvard Business Press.

Kets de Vries, M. F. R. (1979, July/August). Managers can drive their subordinates mad. *Harvard Business Review*, pp. 125–134.

Kets de Vries, M. F. R. (Ed.). (1984). *The Irrational Executive: Psychoanalytic Explorations in Management*. New York: International Universities Press.

Kets de Vries, M. F. R. (Ed.). (1991). *Organizations on the Couch*. San Francisco, CA: Jossey-Bass.

Kets de Vries, M. F. R. (2001). *The Leadership Mystique*. London: FT Prentice Hall.

Kets de Vries, M. F. R. (2005a). Leadership group coaching in action: The zen of creating high performance teams. *Academy of Management Executive*, 19(1): 61–76.

Kets de Vries, M. F. R. (2005b). *Personality Audit: Facilitator Guide*. Fontainebleau: INSEAD Global Leadership Centre.

Kets de Vries, M. F. R. (2005c). *The Global Executive Leadership Inventory Questionnaire: Facilitator's guide*. San Francisco, CA: Pfeiffer.

Kets de Vries, M. F. R. (2006a). *The Leader on the Couch: A Clinical Approach to Changing People and Organizations*. New York, NY: Wiley.

Kets de Vries, M. F. R. (2006b). *Leadership Archetype Questionnaire: Facilitator Guide*. Fontainebleau: INSEAD Global Leadership Centre.

Kets de Vries, M. F. R. (2006c). The eight roles executives play. *Organizational Dynamics*, 36(1): 28–44.

Kets de Vries, M. F. R. (2010a). *The Organizational Culture Audit: Facilitator's Guide*. Fontainebleau: INSEAD Global Leadership Centre.

Kets de Vries, M. F. R. (2010b). *The Organizational Culture Audit: Participant Guide*. Fontainebleau: INSEAD Global Leadership Centre.

Kets de Vries, M. F. R. (2011). *The Hedgehog Effect: The Secrets of Building High Performance Teams*. San Francisco, CA: Jossey-Bass.

Kets de Vries, M. F. R. (2014). *Mindful Leadership Coaching*. London: Palgrave.

Kets de Vries, M. F. R. (2017). *The Global Executive Leadership Mirror: Participant Guide*. Fontainebleau: INSEAD Global Leadership Centre.

Kets de Vries, M. F. R., Korotov, K., and Florent-Treacy, E. (2007). *Coach and Couch: The Psychology of Making Better Leaders*. New York, NY: Palgrave/Macmillan.

Kets de Vries, M. F. R. and Miller, D. (1984). *The Neurotic Organization*. San Francisco, CA: Jossey-Bass.

Kilberg, R. R. (2000). *Executive Coaching*. Washington, DC: American Psychological Association.

Kohut, H. (1971). *The Analysis of the Self*. New York, NY: International Universities Press.

Kohut, H. (1977). *The Restoration of the Self*. Madison, CT: International Universities Press.

Kouzes, J. M. and Posner, B. Z. (1995). *The Leadership Challenge*. San Francisco, CA: Jossey-Bass.

LeDoux, J. (1998). *The Emotional Brain*. London: Weidenfeld & Nicolson.

Levinson, D. J. (1978). *The Seasons of a Man's Life*. New York, NY: Knopf.

Levinson, H. (1972). *Organizational Diagnosis*. Cambridge, MA: Harvard University Press.

Luborsky, L. and Crits-Cristoph, P. (1998). *Understanding Transference: The Core Conflictual Relationship Theme Method*. Washington, DC: American Psychological Association.

Luborsky, L., Crits-Cristoph, P., et al. (1988). *Who Will Benefit from Psychotherapy?* New York: Basic Books.

Malan, D. and Osimo, F. (1992). *Psychodynamics, Training, and Outcome in Brief Psychotherapy*. Oxford: Butterworth Heinemann.

Mann, J. (1973). *Time Limited Psychotherapy*. Cambridge, MA: Harvard University Press.

McCall, M. W. J. and Lombardo, M. M. (1978). *Leadership: Where Else Can We Go?* Durham, NC: Duke University Press.

McCrae, R. R. and Costa, P. T. (1990). *Personality in Adulthood*. New York, NY: Guilford Press.

McCullough Vaillant, L. (1997). *Changing Character*. New York, NY: Basic Books.

McDougall, J. (1985). *Theaters of the Mind: Illusion and Truth on the Psychoanalytic Stage*. London: Routledge.

Menninger, C. (1958). *Theory of Psychoanalytic Technique*. New York, NY: Harper.

Menzies Lyth, I. (1959). The functions of social systems as a defence against anxiety: A report on a study of the nursing service of a general hospital. *Human Relations*, 13: 95–121; reprinted in *Containing Anxiety in Institutions: Selected Essays* (Vol. 1, pp. 43–88). London: Free Association Books, 1988.

Miller, J. G. (1978). *Living Systems*. New York, NY: McGraw-Hill.

Miller, W. R. and Rollnick, S. (2002). *Motivational Interviewing: Preparing People to Change*. New York, NY: Guilford Press.

Millon, T. (2011). *Disorders of Personality: Introducing a DSM/ICD Spectrum from Normal to Abnormal* (3rd ed.). New York, NY: Wiley.

Obholzer, A. and Zagier Roberts, V. (Eds). (1994). *The Unconscious at Work*. London: Routledge.

Ogden, T. H. (1982). *Projective Identification and Psychotherapeutic Technique*. New York, NY: Jason Aronson.

Palmer, S. and Whybrow, A. (2007). *Handbook of Coaching Psychology: A Guide for Practitioners*. London: Routledge.
Pfeffer, J. (1998). *The Human Equation: Building Profits by Putting People First*. Boston, MA: Harvard Business School Press.
Rawson, P. (2002). *Short-term Psychodynamic Psychotherapy: An Analysis of the Key Principles*. London: Karnac.
Rogers, C. R. (1951). *Client-centered Therapy*. Boston, MA: Houghton-Mifflin.
Rosenbaum, M. (1983). *Handbook of Short-term Therapy Groups*. New York, NY: McGraw-Hill.
Salovey, P. and Mayer, J. (1990). Emotional intelligence. *Imagination, Cognition, and Personality*, 9: 185–211.
Scott Rutan, J. and Stone, W. N. (2001). *Psychodynamic Group Psychotherapy*. New York, NY: The Guilford Press.
Schein, E. (1985). *Organizational Culture and Leadership*. San Francisco, CA: Jossey-Bass.
Schon, D. A. (1983). *The Reflective Practitioner: How Professionals Think in Action*. New York, NY: Basic Books.
Seltzery, L. F. (1986). *Paradoxical Strategies in Psychotherapy: A Comprehensive Overview and Guidebook*. New York, NY: Wiley.
Sifneos, P. E. (1979). *Short-term Dynamic Psychotherapy*. Cambridge, MA: Harvard University Press.
Strupp, H. H. and Binder, J. L. (1984). *Psychotherapy in a New Key: A Guide to Time-Limited Dynamic Psychotherapy*. New York, NY: Basic Books.
Vaillant, G. E. (1977). *Adaptation to Life*. Boston, MA: Little Brown.
Watzlawick, P., Jackson, D. D., and Bavelas, J. B. (1968). *Pragmatics of Human Communication: A Study of Interactional Patterns, Pathologies, and Paradoxes*. London: Faber.
Weeks, G. R. and L'Abate, L. (1982). *Paradoxical Psychotherapy: Theory and Practice with Individuals, Couples, and Families*. New York, NY: Brunner/Mazel.
Winnicott, D. W. (1951). *Transitional Objects and Transitional Phenomena. Collected Papers: Through Paediatrics to Psycho-analysis*. London: Tavistock Publications.
Winnicott, D. W. (1971). *Playing and Reality*. New York, NY: Basic Books.
Yalom, I. D. (1970). *The Theory and Practice of Group Psychotherapy*. New York, NY: Basic Books.
Zaleznik, A. (1966). *Human Dilemmas of Leadership*. New York, NY: HarperCollins.

Zaleznik, A. and Kets de Vries, M. F. R. (1975). *Power and the Corporate Mind*. Oxford: Houghton Mifflin.

Index

accountability, responsibility 23, 35, 38, 44, 45, 48, 58, 60, 61, 73, 120, 126, 132, 149, 164, 173
acting/action vi, vii, 2, 3, 14, 20, 58, 71, 73, 74, 84, 93, 96, 101, 102, 104, 106, 127, 143, 157, 158, 173, 176, 183
action trap 183
adaptability/flexibility vii, 12, 13, 25, 38, 87, 90, 92, 97, 148, 172, 185
  of coaches 12
  of leaders 2, 26, 101, 111, 120, 148
  of organizations 2, 110, 113, 121
adaptive and maladaptive inner representations 75
addiction/addictive behaviors 87, 156, 157, 172
Aesop 27
affect/emotional restructuring 72, 74
age of discontinuity 21, 80, 110, 112, 164, 176
"Aha" moments 48, 70, 84

alexithymia 173
anger and anger management vii, 64, 66, 67, 68, 71, 73, 75, 84, 95, 116, 117, 144, 151
anthropological-like observations 55
anticipation 90, 121, 133
anxiety vi, vii, 2, 3, 22, 29, 30, 66, 82, 84, 90, 94, 95, 97, 103, 111, 116, 148, 151, 173. *See also* fear
anxiety about death 159
Archimedes 53
assertiveness 127, 176
assessment instrumentation 54–56, 58, 181. *See also* clinical instrumentation
assessment process 108
assumptions of groups, Bion's basic 28, 29
audit of team dynamics 54
Aurelius, Marcus 1, 27, 184
authenteekos 164
authenticity 13, 38, 39, 161, 164, 176

authentizotic organizations/qualities 165–169
  checklist for 168
  importance of trust 169
  qualities 165, 168, 169
autocratic leadership 126
autonomy vii, 29, 126, 165, 167, 176, 184

bedside, being at the 5, 9
The Beetle and the Pupa (story) 99
behavioral patterns x, 5, 9, 10, 11, 16, 20–26, 66, 69, 70–74, 76, 82, 83, 92, 95, 96, 101, 111, 113, 118, 126, 135, 142, 146, 150, 185. *See also* unconscious/consicous behaviors
behavioral responses 65
belonging, sense of 49, 155, 167, 175, 179, 180
Bion, Wilfred 28, 29, 116
The Black Goat and the White Goat (story) 53
blind spots 10, 38, 55, 141
Bonaparte, Napoleon vi
boredom 94, 156
Bradley, Francis Herbert 89
Brontë, Charlotte 89
Bryan, William Jennings 17
bundlers, in coaching 35
burnout vi, 159, 168, 172
Butler, Joseph 1

Calvin & Hobbes' cartoon 22
career coaching 37
career transition 124
Carroll, Lewis 17
case presentation 144, 152
catalysts of change 49

CEO's defensive structure 73
Cervantes, Miguel de 1, 31
change
  facilitators of 14, 15, 24, 25, 31, 35, 49–51, 56, 58, 62, 70, 72, 76, 85, 86, 91, 94, 96, 102, 103, 105, 106, 108, 112, 117, 118–122, 124, 128, 132, 145, 146–148, 151
  resistance to 14, 23, 71, 86
  tipping points for 14, 16, 48, 49, 85
  see also individual stages of change; organizational change process
change agents/catalysts
  coaches as viii, xiv, 5, 12, 14, 35, 39, 43, 71, 80, 102, 113, 124, 176
  leaders as xiv, 80, 102, 103
"The Challenge of Leadership: Creating Reflective Leaders" program viii, 140
change management xiv, 1, 4, 39
  investigation of human behavior 4
change resistances 20. *See also* resistance to change
Channing, William Ellery 163
charisma, in leaders 112, 127
Chesterton, Gilbert Keith 123
Churchill, Winston 88
Cicero, Marcus Tullius 33, 63
client-centered counseling 13
clinical approach to coaching 4, 5–6, 8, 31, 35, 55, 80, 106. *See also* psychodynamic-systemic methodology
clinical instrumentation 56
clinical paradigm 6, 8–10, 15, 26, 49, 184
  premise 9, 44, 60, 144
  systemic perspective 10, 11
coaches/coaching v, viii, ix, x, xiv, xxi, 5, 14, 20, 25, 26, 34–39,

42, 47, 50–52, 54, 56, 57, 59, 60, 70, 81, 90, 92, 97, 124, 125, 127–137, 145, 146, 168, 173, 181, 183. *See also* executive coaches/coaching and consulting
  as change agents viii, ix, xiv, 5, 12, 15, 35, 39, 43, 71, 80, 102, 113, 124, 176
  benefits of coaching (individual and group) 31, 37, 42, 48–51, 56–60, 80, 91, 112, 124, 132, 183
  challenges of 25, 34, 35, 43, 47, 129, 135, 137, 145
  clinical approach to 4, 5–6, 8, 31, 35, 55, 80, 106
  interventions/intervention techniques xiv, 4, 5, 8, 12–16, 20, 34, 35, 42, 48, 51, 55–57, 59, 70, 81, 91, 125, 130, 135, 136, 140, 146, 147, 184, 187
  objectives of coaching (invdividual and group) 21, 24, 34, 36–39, 103, 129, 130, 133
  qualities of 15, 34, 35, 51, 91, 129, 130, 135, 136
coaching culture 112, 124, 125, 127, 131, 133, 169
  benefits of 50, 125, 128, 131, 132
  modes of adopting 132
cognitive distortions 64, 173
cohesiveness 29
collaboration 36, 43, 46, 47, 50, 62, 109, 128, 135, 138, 141, 166
commitment 26, 46, 47, 50, 51, 86, 87, 102, 104–106, 108, 121, 126, 136, 140, 156, 158, 165, 168, 169
communicators/communication 11, 21, 26, 36, 38, 54, 61, 86, 94, 104, 105, 132, 135, 164, 168, 172
companies ranking 164
competence/competencies 34, 106, 107, 109, 124, 156, 165, 176, 177, 179, 181, 182
complexity x, 3, 26, 35, 51, 59, 113
conceptual frameworks/models viii, 11, 12, 15
conscious and unconscious processes. *See* conscious and unconscious behaviors
confidence vii, x, 34, 92, 96, 110, 119, 130, 169, 185
conflict-avoidant behavior 87
conflict management 36, 44, 47, 48, 141
Confucius 79
conscious and unconscious conceptual processing 96
consciousness 9, 16, 48, 180
consciousness-raising experience 16
constructive conflict/dialogue 111
consulting viii, ix, 20, 35, 127, 137
contagion 50
control vi, 2, 3, 14, 23, 30, 50, 66, 83, 95, 103, 107, 116, 118, 120, 121, 124, 138, 143, 173, 178–180, 184, 185
"C" organizations 2
corporate culture 20, 47, 60, 102, 113, 117, 119, 125. *See also* organizational culture
countertransference reactions 93, 94, 183
courage 26, 132
creativity vii, ix, 18, 25, 26, 30, 36, 38, 44, 50, 57, 92, 96, 111, 125, 128, 133, 136, 144, 165, 174
crystallization of individual's discontent 84, 86, 87, 102
7 Cs of managerial behavior 26
cultural change 126

bottom-up and top-down 129
cultural transformation 113, 125
culture of trust 48, 165, 166
culture surveys 55
customer satisfaction 104, 131

D

dark side of personality 9
Darwin's "survival of the fittest" 166
death, anxiety about 159, 161
decision-making 2–3, 21, 23, 26, 44, 46, 47, 50, 120, 126, 158, 168
defense restructuring 72, 73
defensive/maladaptive behavior patterns 12, 66, 70, 73, 148
defensive reactions/mechanisms vii, x, 4, 7, 10, 14, 22, 30, 38, 55, 66–68, 71–74, 81, 95, 101, 143, 146, 148, 173
360-degree feedback viii, 55, 81, 93, 127, 141, 142
de Montesquieu 63
denial of responsibility 73, 74, 85
dependency 28, 117, 126, 174
dependency assumption (Bion) 28, 30
dependency mode 116, 117, 126
dependency relationships x, 103
developmental imbalance 157
developmental orientation 12
developmental psychology 8
developmental resolutions 175
directive consulting 37
discomfort xiv, xv, 14, 83, 88, 93, 101, 103, 112, 116, 117, 146, 149, 150, 159
displacement 68, 117
distancing/avoidance 81, 83, 104, 117
Don Quixote 31
drivers of change 117, 150
dynamic psychotherapy 8

dysfunctional behavior patterns 16, 20, 21, 26, 49, 67, 71, 73, 75, 79, 83–85, 91, 92, 151
dysfunctional team dynamics 45

E

early childhood experiences and emotions 8, 10, 12, 16, 28, 69, 75
echo chamber 19, 57
elephant in the room x, 4. *See also* undiscussables
Emerson, Ralph Waldo 115, 160
emotional/affect restructuring 72, 74
emotional energy 86
emotional intelligence (EQ) vii, x, xi, 2, 3, 9, 19, 23–25, 38, 43, 46, 94, 119, 124, 127, 136, 142, 144
emotional life in organizations 3
emotional literacy vii, viii, 64, 66, 67, 68, 71, 73, 75, 84, 95, 116, 117, 144, 151. *See also* emotional intelligence (EQ)
emotional outbursts 75
emotional support 119
empathy 3, 8, 18, 30, 49, 71, 90, 94, 112, 134, 146
empowerment, by leaders vii, 105, 118, 126
encouragement, by leaders/organizations 106, 107, 110, 111, 126, 133, 167, 169
"the enemy is us," notion 109
engagement, employee vi, vii, ix, 20, 102, 106, 132, 164–167
Epictetus 181
Epicurus 153
evolutionary psychology 8, 12
executive coaches/coaching viii, xiv, xxi, 10, 24, 34–36, 39, 42, 43, 47, 50, 51, 57, 58, 60, 80, 82, 91, 103, 124, 125, 128, 130,

135, 154, 183. *See also* coaches/coaching and consulting
challenges 25, 34, 43, 47
existential challenges 181
existential psychology 13
experiential learning 91
experimentation 82, 96, 147, 160
exploratory-assertive motivation 176
external coaches 37, 102
external locus of control 120, 121. *See also* personality type

fair pay and benefits 167
family systems theory 8
fear vii, 2, 22, 25, 28, 66, 100, 113, 145, 157. *See also* anxiety
feedback 38, 56, 57, 131
   360-degree viii, 55, 58, 81, 93, 127, 141, 142
   continuous feedback loop 14, 64, 107
   difficulties in giving 51, 57
fight behavior 117
fight–flight assumption (Bion) 28, 29, 116
Fitzgerald, F. Scott 171
flight behavior 117
flights into health or transient highs 146
focal event 83, 85, 86, 108, 110, 151
focus groups 55
"*folie à deux*" collusion 31, 34
follow-up, in coaching 35, 42, 58, 96, 127, 140, 142
Fontaine, Jean de la 17, 53
Fortune's vibrant organizations 164
The Four Bulls and the Lion (story) 27
Freud, Sigmund 8, 9, 171, 172

cognitive and emotional processes 9

Galbraith, John Kenneth 112
Galilei, Galileo 63
Gandhi, Mahatma 79
Global Executive Leadership Inventory (GELI) 56
Global Executive Leadership Mirror (GELM) 56, 127, 141
goal-directedness 29
goals/goal setting 62, 104, 106, 151
group as projective screen 92–93, 95
group coaching 35–37, 42, 48–52, 54, 58–60, 113, 124, 129, 135, 184
   benefits 42, 60
   interventions 42, 48, 51, 55, 56, 59, 70, 81, 140, 147
group dynamics ix, 2, 8, 10, 11, 19, 28, 30, 36, 47, 82, 129, 143, 145, 147
group leadership coaching intervention 59
groupthink processes 36

hardy personality 121. *See also* personality type
healthier organizations 16, 21, 133, 172, 185
healthier individual, characteristics of/becoming a 25, 172–174, 176
helplessness and hopelessness, sense of 28, 84, 86, 94, 12, 151, 152
Hemingway, Ernest 25
Heraclitus 88
high-performance organizations/teams 3, 6, 44, 47, 106, 113, 141, 186

Hippocrates 7, 33
holding environment 93
holistic/macro-orientation, in coaching 30, 34, 37, 39, 56, 123–138
hope v–xi, xiv, 50, 58, 102, 103, 108, 127, 165, 176
hubris 18
Huizinga, Johan 123
human relationships 8, 11, 13, 28, 35, 51, 64, 68–73, 75, 76, 129, 147, 156, 166, 174, 175
  intrapersonal and interpersonal triangles 64
humility 18, 19, 136

individual coaching 36, 38, 42, 51, 137
  benefits 38
  objectives 37
individual executive coaching 82
individual interviews 55
individual psychological well-being 172
individual stages of change/change journey 75, 79–88
  focal event 85
  inner journey 87, 185
  internalization of change 87, 142
  negative emotions 84
  prerequisites of personal change 83–88
  public declaration of intent 58, 83, 108
information systems 168
Inner Theatre Inventory (ITI) 56
inner theater, scripts of x, 9, 55, 71, 72, 96, 174–176, 180, 184
INSEAD viii, 140
insomnia 157, 172
instrumental support 119

intent to change, public expression of 86
intergroup dynamics 10
internal coaches 37
internalization of change 87, 110, 121, 142
internalization process 83, 96
internalized dialogue 185
internal locus of control 120, 121. *See also* personality type
interpersonal conflict 155
intragroup dynamics 10
"I" organizations 2
irrational anger 95
irrational behavior 3–5, 9, 31, 71, 95, 144

James, William 53, 163
Jung, Carl 158

Kakar, Sudhir 139
KDVI (Kets de Vries Institute) viii, ix, x, 141
Kets de Vries, Manfred viii, ix, x, 139
Keynes, John Maynard 22, 23
Kierkegaard, Søren 148
The King's Palace (Zen story) 41
knowledge management 36, 59
knowledge sharing/hoarding 50, 51, 59, 105, 107, 125, 128, 134, 168

Lao Tzu 33
leader–follower relationships 38, 167. *See also* superior–subordinate relationships

leaders/leadership
  becoming/characteristics of
    effective vii, viii, 2, 3, 5, 9, 21,
    23–25, 28, 80, 103–106, 111,
    113, 117, 119, 124, 142, 144,
    164–168, 177, 178
  coaches/coaching viii, xiv, 5, 10,
    20, 25, 37, 47, 50, 51, 54,
    56–59, 124, 125, 128–131,
    134–138, 155, 183
  group (team) coaching 48, 51,
    52, 60, 124
  questionnaires 55, 142
  teams vii, ix, 43, 48–52, 54, 56,
    59, 130
Leader Archetype Questionnaire
  (LAQ) 56, 127
leaders in orbit 23
learning organization/continuous
  learning ix, 39, 44, 82, 112,
  125, 128, 133, 138, 142, 146,
  147, 164, 169, 177
legacy coaching 37
legacy creation 38, 159, 177
letting go, process of 115–122
life balance 127, 158, 168
life case study 140, 141, 145
life coaching 35, 37, 124
listening 31, 38, 43, 49, 90, 95, 96,
  119, 128, 141, 152, 167, 169,
  181, 183, 185
listen with the third ear 93–96
loneliness 29, 151, 157
loss/losses 22, 73, 104, 117, 154,
  155, 157, 174

macho culture 126
macro developmental process of
  organizations 124
macro/holistic perspective in
  coaching 30, 34, 37, 56,
  123–138

madness 30, 31, 34
major life themes 153–161
  addiction/addicitve behaviors 156
  boredom 156
  developmental imbalance 157
  interpersonal conflict 155, 156
  life balance 158. *See also*
    work–life balance; well-lived
    life
  loss 154
  primacy of meaning 158, 159. *See
    also* meaningful life
Martial 97
meaningful life 13, 38, 44, 48, 120,
  158–161, 164, 165, 167, 168,
  176–180. *See also* well-lived
  life
meaning in life 178
  five pillars 180, 181
  pillars of 179
Meaning in Life Questionnaire 180,
  182
Melville, Henry 27
mental well-being 76, 84, 172
mentoring 133, 168
micro-managers 23
mirror neurons 49, 94
mood management 67
morale 75, 102, 128, 169
morosoph or wise fool 64
motivation v, ix, 9, 13, 14, 21, 25,
  29, 87, 101, 102, 104, 106,
  112, 119, 125, 133, 137, 147,
  151, 167, 169, 174, 175, 176,
  178
motivational interviewing 8, 13
motivational need systems 9,
  174–177
mourning the past 107, 110, 117,
  118
mutual coaching 141
mutual identification 49

N

Nansen, Fridtof 115
narcissistic behavior/narcissistic thinking 18, 19, 23
narcissism/egotistical behavior in leaders 19, 20
Nasruddin and the Finding of Joy (Sufi story) 89
negative emotions 83, 84
negative self-concept 152
networking 2, 36, 42, 113, 125, 133, 169
neuroscience 8, 13
Newton, Isaac 27
Nietzsche, Friedrich 123
The Nobleman and the Zen Master (Zen story) 7
Nobody (Sufi story) 123

O

object relations theory 8
on-boarding coaching 37
one-to-one coaching 35, 146
open questioning 58, 67. *See also* Socratic approach to leadership coaching
optimism v, vii, x, 165
organizational anxieties, dealing with 30
organizational change process 101, 107
  carrying out transformation 105
  constructive team environment, creating 113
  cultural transformation 113, 125
  dependency relationships x, 103
  emotional support 119
  employee participation and involvement 106
  fight or flight mode 116
  hardiness factor 121
  hope, creation of 103
  locus of control 120, 121
  means of motivation and participation 104
  redefining phase
  role of change agents 80, 102
  role of leadership 110, 127
  shared mind-set, development of 102
  social support for 118, 119
  transforming past 110
  visible improvements 106
organizational clinicians 12, 172
organizational culture 10, 39, 55–57, 106, 111, 112, 124, 126, 132, 133, 141, 156, 165, 166, 169. *See also* corporate culture
  influencing factors 124, 125, 131
  values 125, 133, 166
Organizational Culture Audit (OCA) 56
organizational detectives 9, 16
  clients as 16
  coaches as 9
organizational dynamics, study of psychodynamic-systemic clinical approach 15
organizational flexibility vii
organizational growth 9, 44, 126, 132
organizational leadership 131, 136, 177
organizational leadership coaching
  assessment of intervention 137
  benefits of 133
  objectives of 131
  Socratic approach 58, 136
Orwell, George 171
Ovid 99
ownership/responsibility vii, 21, 38, 120, 137, 160, 173

P

pairing assumption (Bion) 28, 29
paradoxical intervention 8, 14

paralysis vi, 23, 83, 84, 95. *See also* stuck, experience of being
past relationships/experiences 70
  link with present 12, 16, 70, 71, 83, 86, 95, 148, 152
pathological behavior 96
pathological regressive processes 28
performance coaching 37, 124
personal/individual growth and development vi, xi, 9, 96, 124, 126, 132, 167–8, 177, 184, 185
The Personality Audit (PA) 56, 142
personality tests 55, 142
personality type 118
personal relationships 28, 35, 129, 156
The Pike's Dilemma (story) 79
play, importance of 24, 25, 92, 93, 97, 174, 176
Poe, Edgar Allan 153
positive change 6, 39, 49, 112, 120
positive environments/positivity ix, 50, 64, 76, 96, 117, 120, 121, 171, 174
positive outcome 29, 97, 146
power dynamics 20, 44–46, 102
Power Dynamics (story) 17
powerholders 20, 101, 103, 105, 111, 132
power to control 116
primacy of meaning 158
primary caretakers 69
privileged relationships 69
problem-solving exercise 58
projection 30, 67, 73
projective identification 94
Proust, Marcel 7
pseudo-team behavior 43
psychoanalysis/psychoanalytic theory 8, 9, 28
psychoanalytically oriented clinical paradigm 8
psychodynamics of groups 28
Bion's basic assumptions 28
psychodynamic-systemic methodology v, 16, 12, 15, 145, 184. *See also* clinical approach to coaching
psychological mindedness 140, 148
psychosomatic response 65, 68
psychotherapy 136
public declaration of intent 58, 83, 86–87, 88, 108. *See also* individual stages of change
purpose, sense of 13, 143, 159, 166, 178–181

Q

qualitative assessment of coaching 138

R

rational behavior 3–5, 9
readiness to change 87, 140
receptivity to change 148
reciprocal coaching 125, 128
recognition 74, 135, 165, 167, 184
Recollections of a Younger Self (story) 1
reflective leaders/leadership viii–x, xi, 50, 181, 184
reflective practitioners 16, 183
reframing x, 90, 155, 174
rehearsal 90
reinvention process 25
repression 48, 49, 67, 68, 73
resilience vi, ix, 8, 121, 122, 127
resistance to change 14, 19, 20–23, 35, 39, 56, 71, 79, 80, 82, 83, 85, 86, 100, 101, 104, 105, 107, 112, 117, 133, 140, 146, 150
resistance judo 13
reward structures 57, 105, 107, 128, 134, 167

rigidification 111, 112
ritualistic behavior 116
role assignments 44
Roosevelt, Theodore 122
Rúmí, Jalálu'ddín 41, 99, 153

S

safety 47, 50, 71, 92, 166
Saint-Exupéry, Antoine de 89
Schweitzer, Albert 160
screen memory 86
secondary gains 150
security 22, 47, 119
self-affirmation 76, 176
self-awareness vii, viii, 24, 135, 174, 184
self-centered people 18, 145
self-confidence 18, 44, 58, 120
self-confident 26, 38
self-control 65, 120, 184
self-determination 13, 178
self-direction 184
self-disclosure 48, 49, 185. *See also* letting go
self-discovery process 24, 110, 141, 147, 157, 185, 186
self-esteem 75, 90, 97, 119, 124, 127, 172, 175
self-fulfilling prophecy 75, 76
self-image 75
self-knowledge vii, 24, 25, 87
self-leadership development 125
self-perception 55, 75
  restructuring 72, 73, 75
self-understanding 13, 16, 23, 44, 71, 90, 93, 95
Seneca 152
sense making 152, 154
Shakespeare, William 64
shame and guilt 58, 66, 158
shared mind-set 102
short-term dynamic psychotherapy 12, 146, 147

signalling events 48
A Sign for Prosperity (Zen story) 153
silo-type behavior 36, 46, 60, 113
simulations/role-play viii, 55, 75, 90
small wins 106
Smith, Sydney 53
social defenses 30
social defense mechanisms. *See* defensive reactions
social support 58, 71, 87, 118, 119, 166, 174
Socrates 25
Socratic approach to leadership coaching 58, 134–137
Socratic coaches 136
soft skills 3, 43
Sophocles 7, 47
speech and language evolution 94
splitters, in coaching 35
splitting 29, 30, 35, 67
Stanton, Elizabeth Cady 99
storytelling 49, 58, 70, 96, 141, 152, 160, 181. *See also* listening
strategic dialogue 107, 108, 110, 111
stress factors of organization 102
stressors, internal and external 185
stress/stressors vi, 72, 73, 81, 82, 84, 97, 101, 103, 118, 121, 124, 127, 151, 159, 172, 185
  workplace stress vi, 38, 101, 102, 117, 121, 172
stuck, experience of being viii, xv, 11, 24, 88, 110, 143. *See also* paralysis
succession planning 46, 128, 133. *See also* power dynamics
sunk costs 22
superior–subordinate relationships 38, 57, 60
support network 87, 156, 174
survival mechanisms 73
systems theory 10, 11

team coaching 51, 59, 60, 134
team dynamics x, 42, 44, 54–56, 60
team dysfunctionality 24, 34, 45. *See also* dysfunctional team dynamics
team leadership development process 56
teams/teamwork 42, 43, 56, 61, 113, 134, 164, 166
  conflict in 29, 36, 43, 45, 46, 48, 49, 51, 56, 61, 95
  dynamics of. *See* team dynamics
  dysfunctionality in. *See* team dysfunctionality
  effectiveness of 42–46, 47, 48, 55, 59, 60, 112
teddy bear factor 119
tipping points of change 14, 16, 48, 49, 82, 85, 100, 151, 158
Tolstoy, Leo 39
toxic working environment 20, 39
traditional organizations 2
transcendence 91, 179, 180
transferential reactions 71, 91, 183
transferential relationships/transference 68–70, 95
transformative events, staging 107, 108
  benefits of 108, 110
  staging 106, 107, 109
transitional space 92, 93, 133, 136, 147. *See also* safe space
transition coaching 37
The Traveler and the Wise Man (Sufi story) 63
Travelling (Zen story) 163
triangle of conflict 66–68, 72, 73
  defensive/maladaptive behavior patterns 66
triangles of insight 12, 63–77
triangle of mental life 9, 64–70
  behavioral responses 65
  cognitive aspect 64
  emotional responses 64, 70
triangle of relationships 68–70, 72, 73
triangles of insight 12, 72, 73, 80
trust x, 5, 37, 38, 43, 47, 48, 59, 62, 76, 93, 113, 119, 125, 128–130, 132, 136, 164, 166–169, 183, 185
turf fights 46, 102, 113, 117
Twain, Mark 139, 163
Two Monks and the King (Zen story) 33
The Two Snakes (story) xiii
The Two Travelers and the Stream (Zen story) 115

unconscious/consicous behaviors x, 3, 4, 9, 10, 12, 14, 16, 20, 28, 55, 74, 80, 83, 91, 93, 129, 135, 145, 146, 184. *See also* behavioral patterns
undiscussables x, 4, 36, 45, 48, 54, 107, 136
unity 16, 29, 42, 62, 134, 180
unlearning xiv, 23

Valéry, Paul 115
values ix, 24, 43, 44, 56, 104, 105, 108, 111, 118, 125, 128, 133–135, 164, 166, 168, 169, 175, 180, 183
values-based mission statement 166
vicarious learning 48, 49, 58
virtual teams 59, 61, 113
vision 4
vulnerability vii, 148

W

well-lived life xv, 13, 25, 97, 135, 147, 152, 178, 179, 185. *See also* meaningful life
Wilde, Oscar 101
willingness 12, 24, 25, 29, 49, 59, 85, 87, 101, 147
willingness to change 24, 25, 30, 101, 147
Wilson, Harold xv
Wilson, Woodrow 79
work environment 166, 169
work–life balance 38, 124, 165, 172, 181
working relationships 37, 131, 135

X

Xenophanes 26
Xunzi 138

Y

Yes (story) 171
The Young Man and the Old Man (story) 139

Z

zero-sum game mindset 46
zoteekos 164, 165

GPSR Compliance

The European Union's (EU) General Product Safety Regulation (GPSR) is a set of rules that requires consumer products to be safe and our obligations to ensure this.

If you have any concerns about our products, you can contact us on

ProductSafety@springernature.com

In case Publisher is established outside the EU, the EU authorized representative is:

Springer Nature Customer Service Center GmbH
Europaplatz 3
69115 Heidelberg, Germany

www.ingramcontent.com/pod-product-compliance
Lightning Source LLC
LaVergne TN
LVHW011008250326
834688LV00004B/138